FISH HOUSE

Book of Fish

D1367095

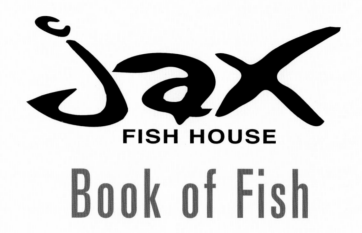

Book of Fish

DAVE QUERY AND JILL ZEH RICHTER

PRUETT

PRUETT PUBLISHING COMPANY
BOULDER, COLORADO

Pruett Publishing Company
7464 Arapahoe Road, Suite A9
Boulder, Colorado 80303
www.pruettpublishing.com

Printed in China

11 10 09 08 07 06 05 04 03 02   5 4 3 2 1

        Library of Congress Cataloging-in-Publication Data
Query, Dave.
    Jax Fish House book of fish / Dave Query and Jill Zeh Richter.
        p. cm.
    Includes bibliographical references and index.
    ISBN 0-87108-921-1 (alk. paper)
    1. Cookery (Fish) 2. JAX Fish House. I. Richter, Jill Zeh. II. Title.

    TX747 .Q47 2002
    641.6′92--dc21   2002022457

Book design by Studio Signorella (www.signorella.com)
Photography by Bill Cooley (www.cooleyimages.com)
Food styling by Jill Zeh Richter
India-ink fish drawings by John Carlson
Ceramic fish sculptures featured on pages 29 and 110 by Chris Winding
Paintings featured on pages 8 and 81 by Sonny Smith
Painted fish featured on page 38 by Craig Marshall
Mermaid sculpture/painting featured on page 82 by Gayle Crites
Painting featured on page 107 by Kevan Krasnoff

Contents

VII

Preface

Imagine if your business idea is to throw a party in your house every single night of the week, every single week of the year, year after year. Everyday, you do all the things you do to get ready for a party. You line out the music you know your friends love, polish the silverware, check the temperature, create the most delicious food, and have crisp cold cocktails ready for immediate consumption. You clean every square inch of your house, wondering how it could get dirty after such a thorough cleaning just the day before. You assemble a staff of really intelligent friends to help you service the nightly soiree and try to explain to them the purpose for throwing this party in hopes that they will embrace your idea as their own.

In your kitchen you have a collection of individuals whose only mission each day is to do their jobs with more skill and integrity than anyone else on the planet. Every day at 4:00 P.M. your friends start to show up, and by 5:30 you have many more friends than you expected and they are actually waiting with their names on a list for a chance to sit at a table at your party. During the party you are constantly asking your friends how they are doing and if there is anything they need that isn't within their reach. As the party winds down, you walk each guest to your front door, thanking them so much for coming to your party, wishing them a safe drive home, and inviting them back tomorrow night for yet another party. Same time, same place. That is what we do at our restaurants every single day.

The plan was to open a small fish house on Pearl Street because Boulder didn't have one. The culture and the success that would follow were totally unexpected. The Denver JAX opened soon after in a funky old building that Jack Kerouac lived in and Tom Waits sang about. Being fifteen hundred miles from the nearest ocean made the challenge that much harder. The commitment early on was for simple food influenced by the travels of my wife and mine after we both graduated from the Culinary Institute of America, her Louisiana childhood, and my love for all things fish, especially raw. While there are still a few hints of southern food, the menus have been expanded wide open by the few chefs who have taken the helm of these kitchens over the years.

Running a successful fish house is like juggling ice cubes on a hot day: You have to be quick and precise, sourcing new oysters, being the home of all things seasonal, and keeping the chalk board constantly fresh in an effort to do your very best and serve an incredibly fresh product smack in the middle of the Rocky Mountains. A big airport with constant flights from all coasts of the United States keeps us flush with the freshy-fresh product. This book is a sampling of the style of food that you would find on any night at JAX. It is random and eclectic, much like the food we serve and the overall experience our diners encounter. We hope that you find these recipes delicious and that we have given you one small tool to throw a great party of your own and cook some fabulous food.

Dave Query
Chef/Owner

We didn't want to write a typical cookbook. JAX restaurants are not typical. So we thought it might be best to write a little explanation of how we set this cookbook up. We wanted to give you a sampling of the best dishes, or entire "plates," that we have created at JAX over the years. That meant compiling a lot of menus and specials and pulling out all the shining stars. We were also thinking there are a lot of fish out there and not everyone is familiar with all of them, so we wanted to pack a lot of fish information in as well.

So this is what we did to fit them into a book.

The fish are alphabetized. The more popular types of fish have several plates, and the less known and less available types usually only got one. Each plate has several recipes. There is one recipe for how to cook the fish, one for the sauce that goes with it, and another for the potatoes, rice, or pasta, and any condiments, so you can replicate the exact dish that is served in the restaurant.

There is a lot of gray area when writing recipes. When no specific size of vegetable is noted, we mean an average-size onion or lemon. If the bunches of cilantro or parsley are unusually large or small the day you are shopping, take that into consideration. When we don't mention the amount of salt and pepper, use enough for seasoning. We always use kosher salt, and white pepper is definitely better for seasoning fish. All herbs are fresh unless noted. If a recipe calls for vegetable oil, we mean any except olive, which would overpower the flavor of that particular dish. When plating entrées, we included the ounce measurements as well as cups for sauces because it is much easier to use a two-, four-, or six-ounce ladle to put sauce on a plate than a measuring cup.

The whole point is to have fun with this book. Don't stress about how many spears are in a bunch of asparagus, how much juice is in one lemon, or if you have a little leftover sauce. Turn the music up loud, start cooking, and get ready for your party.

Jill Zeh Richter
Chef

Acknowledgments

This book is dedicated to a lot of people. First to Amy, for talking us into putting the bar in the middle, for constant menu advice in the early years, and so many, many other things. To the many original JAX-Boulder employees who were paramount in the creation and continued maintenance of the culture, especially Ray, Kathy, Big Daddy, Analisa, Alison, Dewi, Peter, Hicks, Klinker, Jessie M., Janine, Marci, Rayme, Brendan, Pflumy, Mer, Julian, Benham, Iva, Rachel, R2, Brett, and the Denver crew of Timothy Dale, Jon, Wing Ding, Lin, Jane, Kristen, Mitch, Juliette, Gina, KO, Matty, Mark V, Yoshi, She-lah, Ophelia, Jorge, and to the memories of Chris Spiller and Ian Baird and their contagious smiles. To Robin for making all the cool things look so . . . cool.

To the chefs who have poured their hearts and lives into running these kitchens over the years: Jamey Fader, Chris Blackwood, Christopher Wellman, Paul Schutt, Jason Dascoli, and Chef Rog (who has tasted everything a million times at the Boulder restaurant and has checked in even more seafood deliveries).

To Jill Richter, who manned (womaned) the helm of the kitchen at JAX-Denver not once but twice, pregnant, smiling, and tired. She has worked incredibly hard and has carried the proverbial torch in getting this book into your hands.

To Paul Packer and the entire crew at Northeast Seafood, where we purchase 100 percent of everything we serve that lives in water. Their relentless commitment to quality has helped us to continually raise the bar on our own. To my partners who believed in JAX and continue to be great friends and supporters.

To Glenn and Val who have kept us in line, in focus, and on track.

To my children, Matt, Harry, and Z, who will be in the dish hole in the not-too-distant future. And last, I dedicate this book to an incredible collection of customers—without your loyalty, generosity, support, feedback, and appreciation for what we do, these restaurants would be no fun at all. Cheers.

Dave Query

JAX Cooking Methods

Although there are many ways to cook a fish, at JAX we primarily use four cooking methods, pan searing, pan roasting, grilling, and deep frying. To properly cook the following recipes, we thought it would be best to describe what we mean by these cooking methods.

PAN SEARING is a method of sauténg in which items are cooked quickly in a small amount of hot fat or oil in a pan on top of the range. Fish can be a delicate item to cook. Although fish varies greatly in texture and flavor, pan searing seems to work well for many types. Thin cuts, which are delicate, benefit from this cooking method by sealing in juices and finishing the process in a matter of minutes.

PAN ROASTING is a form of sautéing in which you brown the fish on one side, turn it over, and place it in a hot oven to finish cooking. This cooking method works well for thicker cuts of fish because it enables you to cook the fish all the way through without burning it on one side. The secret to both sautéing and pan roasting is to make sure the oil and pan are very hot before you add the fish. Too much heat will cause the oil to flame and will affect the taste of the oil and the finished product. Be careful with your temperatures. An added benefit from sautéing and pan roasting is making a pan sauce from the browned bits found in the bottom of the pan.

GRILLING is a method in which items are cooked over a radiant heat source: gas, charcoal, electricity, or wood. Grilling works best on the more dense, meaty types of fish—tuna, mahi mahi, salmon, swordfish, trout, and opah, for example. Shellfish is also great on the grill, such as clams, mussels, lobster, and shrimp. Grilling fish is a delicate operation; if the grill surface isn't clean or well seasoned (oiled) or hot enough, the fish may stick and you will lose part of it in the fire. If you overcook the fish, it will be very dry. Also, you must let the fish cook long enough on one side before trying to turn it over. As the fish cooks, the proteins coagulate—you can actually watch the fish shrink in size; it is losing water content as it cooks. If you try to pick up the fish with tongs or a spatula and it sticks to the grill, wait one to two more minutes and try again. If the grill is clean and oiled and hot, the fish should release from the cooking surface.

Another point to remember when grilling fish is that it does not have to stay directly over the heat source the whole time it is cooking. It is comparable to pan roasting. First, grill the outside of the fish over direct heat to seal in the juices and then move the fish to another part of the grill and cover it to let it finish roasting on the grill. This is a great way to avoid charring the outside of the thicker cuts of fish, which can take some time to cook all the way through.

DEEP FRYING is a cooking method in which food is submerged in hot oil. Seafood is first coated with flour, then egg wash, and then bread crumbs or cornmeal. We did not specify the amounts of oil for frying in the recipes because we don't know what size fryer you have! Please just refer to the manufacturer's instructions.

Ingredients

Here are some explanations of ingredients that may be unfamiliar in this book. In the back of the book are two more informational sections. One is a list of cooking terms and equipment defined, and the other is a list of Web sites where you can find some of those hard-to-find ingredients.

Anaheim chili pepper—this widely available pepper is mild, green, long, and narrow.

ancho chili powder—dried ground poblano peppers, which are large, thin-skinned, dark green, mild chilies.

andouille—a type of spicy, smoked pork sausage used in creole cooking.

Asiago cheese—similar to Parmesan, it is a semi-firm Italian cheese made from cow's milk.

Atomic Horseradish—a brand we use at JAX that is much more powerful than your average horseradish.

beluga lentils—small black lentils that look similar to beluga caviar.

bird peppers—similar to pequins; these tiny, dried Thai peppers are very spicy.

cedar planks—untreated cedar planks can be found in hardware stores or specialty food stores; they are great to grill food on to impart a smoky flavor.

chanterelles—trumpet-shaped wild mushrooms, ranging in color from golden to orange-brown. Available fresh in fall.

chili/chile—there are over two hundred varieties of peppers, indigenous to Mexico. As a general rule, the smaller they are the spicier they are.

Chimayo chili powder—Chimayo is a little town in New Mexico known for its chilies. If you can't find Chimayo, use red chili powder.

chipotle chilies in adobo sauce—dried, smoked jalapeños in a piquant sauce made from ground chilies, herbs, and vinegar.

Cholula—a spicy, vinegary tomato hot sauce. Cholula is a brand name.

curry paste—usually red or green, a mixture of mashed chilies, ghee (clarified butter), curry powder, and vinegar.

filé powder—ground sassafras leaves, used as a thickening agent in southern stews like gumbo and étouffée.

kosher salt—additive-free, coarse-grained salt.

leeks—related to garlic and onion families, they look like giant green onions, very sweet and subtly flavored; be sure to wash between the layers to remove any grit.

mafaldina pasta—skinny lasagna noodles.

miso paste—mashed and fermented soybeans, ranging in color from white, which is mild, to red, which is strong and aged; it is rich in B vitamins and protein.

pancetta—an Italian-rolled bacon that has not been smoked.

peperoncini—a sweet and hot pickled pepper.

pickled ginger—shaved ginger that has been preserved in sweet vinegar; it can be white or pink in color.

poblano chili pepper—usually dark green when you find them at the grocery store, these two- to three-inch-wide and four- to five-inch-long triangular-shaped chilies can also turn reddish-brown in color.

prosciutto—dry, aged Italian ham that has not been smoked but has been pressed for a firmer texture; it is usually sold in very thin slices.

queso fresco—a semi-soft mild Mexican cheese that literally means "fresh cheese," similar to farmer cheese.

rice noodles—thin white noodles made from rice flour, which can be fried or soaked in hot water before serving.

sambal—Indonesian and Malaysian condiment made from chilies, brown sugar, and salt.

serrano chili pepper—small red or yellow pepper that is very hot.

shallots—part of the green onion family; a small, sweet, pink onion that is very mild in flavor.

soba noodles—Japanese noodles made from buckwheat flour, usually dark brown in color.

sushi rice—short-grained rice that tends to stick together after cooking because of its high starch content.

sweet soy sauce—also called kecap manis, is Indonesian and similar to soy sauce but much thicker, more syrupy, and sweetened with palm sugar and flavored with garlic and star anise.

tamarind—also known as Indian date, it grows as a long pod found in trees in Asia and northern Africa and has a sour lemony flavor; it is used much like lemons and can be found fresh, in paste form, or as a syrup.

udon noodles—fat Japanese noodles made from wheat or corn flour; they can be found fresh in the refrigerated section of most Asian groceries or dried.

wasabi—a very hot Japanese horseradish, usually green in color, available in paste or powdered form.

wasabi tobiko—a fine-grained caviar from flying-fish roe, it is seasoned with wasabi powder.

whole-grain mustard—prepared mustard in which whole brown mustard seeds have not been pureed.

Buying Fish

Freshness, Quality, and Buying

It used to be that if you didn't live on a coast, there wasn't fresh seafood available. Some people still believe that's true; at JAX we know it's not true. With both of our restaurants in Colorado—a landlocked state—we receive great-quality seafood every day. Yes, every day. We are lucky. We order it at night, and the next morning... there it is, glistening in the ice. The fact is, fresh seafood is available every day everywhere; you just need to know how to look for it.

Many of the cookbooks say the same things: Talk to your local fishmonger (who uses that word anymore?), look for bright eyes and red gills, and when you touch the fish the flesh should bounce back, not leave an impression. Helloooo . . . have these people been to a supermarket lately? The fish is almost always filleted, there are no bright eyes or gills to look at (unless you're buying trout—those are sometimes still sold whole), and you can't touch the fish because it's behind glass. Who wants a bunch of people touching the fish you're buying anyway? So unless you live in Seattle and go to the fish market there, the criteria have changed.

Who to Buy Fish From

Ask the folks behind the counter if it's fresh or frozen—they will usually be honest. Ask them a question about fish. Where did the salmon come from? Is it farm raised or wild? If they stammer, you may want to change stores. Talk to them about the fish. If they know their stuff, they won't mind the questions, and they may even start to tip you off about what looks the best that day. Another good idea is to special order something that they don't have in the case—then you know it will be fresh.

What Fish to Buy

Buy whatever you like; most recipes in this book are geared for any fish. We just wanted to give you some ideas for fish you may not have cooked before. But if your favorite fish isn't in this book, buy it anyway and pick a recipe that has a similar type of fish and that looks good to you—it will be a fabulous combination.

Where to Buy Fish

Find a store that sells a lot of fish and where you won't find the same fish sitting in the case behind the glass all week. Go in the store in the evening, after the guys who sell the fish go home. Did they lay a big piece of plastic wrap over the fish still in the case? Or did they go to the trouble of taking it out of the case, wrapping it up, melting the old ice, and putting it in the cooler overnight?

When to Buy Fish

Fish doesn't have the shelf life that other meats do. Don't let it sit in your refrigerator for more than twenty-four hours; and if it's live, like mussels, clams, or lobsters, cook it the day you buy it.

Why Buy Fish

Don't you read the paper? Fish is good for your heart and your brain, and we are all sick of chicken anyway.

Pantry

Here are some basic items to help prepare the dishes on the following pages:

Beurre Blanc

Yield: 1 cup

This is a great sauce to add moisture to any fish. It is an emulsion sauce (which means you are suspending a fat in a liquid), a delicate sauce that may not hold together (not stay emulsified) if its temperature gets too hot or too cold. It must be kept warm (110°F) after making, until serving, to keep the proper consistency.

1 tablespoon minced shallots
$\frac{1}{4}$ cup white wine
1 tablespoon lemon juice
2 tablespoons heavy cream
6 ounces (1 1/4 sticks) butter, diced the size of lima beans

In a small sauté pan over medium-high heat, combine shallots, wine, and lemon juice. Reduce until there is almost no liquid left in the pan, being careful not to let the shallots burn; reduce heat as necessary. Add heavy cream and let reduce by one-half, 1 to 2 minutes. Reduce heat to very low. Slowly whisk in the butter, one or two pieces at a time, adding more when each piece has melted. The sauce should become slightly thickened and very blond in color. Pour sauce into a squeeze tube and place in a pot of warm water. It can be held this way for about an hour.

Cocktail Sauce

Yield: 3 1/2 cups

- $\frac{1}{2}$ cup horseradish
- 2 tablespoons lemon juice
- 2 teaspoons Cholula
- 2 teaspoons dry mustard
- $\frac{1}{2}$ teaspoon kosher salt
- $\frac{1}{2}$ teaspoon black pepper
- 2 cups ketchup
- $1\frac{1}{3}$ cups chili sauce

Whisk all ingredients together in a small bowl. Cover and refrigerate.

Crème Fraîche

Yield: 1 1/4 cups

You are making the French version of sour cream. It will be the consistency of lightly whipped cream.

- 1 cup heavy cream
- $\frac{1}{4}$ cup buttermilk

Whisk ingredients together and blend thoroughly. Place mixture uncovered in a warm spot (on top of the fridge) for 24 hours. Then cover and refrigerate for 24 hours more. Whisk lightly and it is ready to use.

Fish Stock

Yield: 8 cups

You should be able to find fish bones at your local grocer, but you may have to order them a day ahead. Be sure to use cold water when making fish stock. Hot water cooks the blood in the bones too quickly. Cold water lets the flavor seep out gradually. Oily bones like those in salmon will produce a heavier-scented stock. White fish bones are recommended. Also, for those of you who are "time challenged," you can substitute half clam juice and half water where a recipe calls for fish stock.

- 1 pound fish bones
- 2 lemons, cut in half
- 1 diced onion
- 1 chopped leek
- 3 stalks diced celery
- 1 bunch coarsely chopped parsley
- 8 cups cold water

Place all ingredients in a stockpot. Bring to a boil. Reduce heat to simmer. Skim surface to remove any foam (impurities) as necessary. Cook for 45 minutes. Strain out bones and vegetables. Reserve liquid as stock. You may want to freeze leftover stock in 2-cup batches to use at a later time.

JAX Rice

Yield: 2 cups

- 1 tablespoon olive oil
- $\frac{1}{4}$ cup finely diced onion
- 1 tablespoon butter
- 1 cup long-grain white rice
- 1 teaspoon minced thyme
- 1 teaspoon minced oregano
- $1\frac{1}{2}$ cups water

Heat oil in heavy 2-quart saucepan over medium-high heat. Add onion and sauté until translucent, approximately 12 to 15 minutes. Add butter, rice, thyme, and oregano and sauté another 2 minutes. Add water and bring to a boil. Reduce heat to low and cover. Simmer 20 to 30 minutes, until rice is tender and has absorbed all the water.

Roasted Garlic or Shallots and Oil

Yield: 1 cup oil and 3/4 cup mashed or pureed garlic or shallots

Roasted garlic and shallots and their oils are great to use when cooking just about anything!

- **1 cup whole, peeled cloves of garlic or shallots**
- **1 cup olive oil**

Preheat oven to 325°F. Place garlic or shallots in an oven-proof dish and add oil. Place in oven and roast until garlic or shallots are tender, about 45 minutes to an hour. Remove from oven and let cool. Drain and reserve oil.

TO MAKE ROASTED GARLIC OR SHALLOT PASTE: Garlic cloves should be soft enough to mash with the side of your French knife. Shallots are easier to puree in a food processor. It may be necessary to add a little oil back into the puree to smooth it out.

Toasted Flour

Yield: 1 cup

Use this to thicken gumbo, étouffée, and Brunswick stew.

- **1 cup flour**

Preheat oven to 325°F. Spread flour in a thin layer on a sheet tray. Toast flour in the oven until it is light brown in color, approximately 15 to 20 minutes. It will be necessary to stir the flour with a metal spatula a couple of times for uniform toasting, as the edges will darken faster than the center. Remove from oven and let cool. Sift cool flour through a strainer to remove any lumps created while toasting.

3

Yield: 6 servings

Salmon can be substituted if char is not available.

- ½ cup ground walnuts
- 1 tablespoon flour
- 1 tablespoon minced garlic
- 1 tablespoon minced shallots
- ½ teaspoon kosher salt
- ½ teaspoon white pepper
- 2¼ pounds arctic char, cut into 6 pieces
- 2 tablespoons olive oil

Preheat oven to 400°F. Mix together walnuts, flour, garlic, shallots, salt, and pepper. Gently press topside of each char fillet into walnut mixture and set fillets on one large plate. Place an oven-safe sauté pan over medium-high heat. Add oil to pan; don't let oil get too hot or walnuts will burn. Place fillets in pan, walnut side down. Let cook 2 to 3 minutes. Walnuts should toast to golden brown. Reduce heat to medium; keep checking pan to be sure that walnuts are not burning. Turn fillets over, place pan in oven, and roast another 2 to 3 minutes depending on thickness of the fillets and desired doneness.

 TO PLATE: *Place a square of Shiitake Bread Pudding in six shallow serving bowls. Lay fillets on top of bread pudding. Ladle about 1/2 cup of Acorn Squash Broth over each fillet. Top with 1/3 cup Pear Chutney.*

Shiitake Bread Pudding

Yield: 6 servings

If the baguettes are stale, mix them with the eggs and half-and-half ahead of time to let the bread soak up the liquid, then add the remaining ingredients and bake just before serving.

- 2 baguettes, cut into 1/2- to 1-inch cubes
- 1 cup finely diced onion
- 1 cup finely diced celery
- 1 cup finely diced carrot
- 2 cups julienne shiitake mushrooms
- 4 beaten eggs
- 3 cups half-and-half
- 1 teaspoon kosher salt
- ½ teaspoon freshly ground black pepper

Preheat oven to 375°F. Place bread cubes in a large bowl. Add onion, celery, carrot, and mushrooms. In another large bowl, whisk together eggs, half-and-half, salt, and pepper. Pour egg mixture over bread and vegetables; stir well to saturate bread cubes evenly, then pour into an ungreased 13 x 9 x 2-inch baking dish. Cover with foil and bake for 45 minutes. Remove foil and bake approximately 15 more minutes to brown the top. When done, bread pudding should be firm in center. It will puff up in the oven and deflate when cooling. Let rest 15 minutes. Cut into 6 portions.

Acorn Squash Broth

Yield: 3 cups, 6 servings

For a great soup, place leftover onion, carrot, celery, and squash mixture in a blender, add leftover broth and a little stock or water, and puree. Reheat and season to taste with salt and pepper.

- 1 halved and seeded acorn squash
- 2 tablespoons melted butter
- 2 tablespoons honey
- 2 tablespoons brown sugar
- $\frac{1}{8}$ teaspoon cinnamon
- 1 zested and juiced lemon
- 2 tablespoons olive oil
- 1 cup diced onion
- 1 cup diced celery
- 1 cup diced carrots
- $\frac{1}{4}$ cup brandy
- 4 cups fish stock (p. 2)
- 1 teaspoon kosher salt
- 1 teaspoon white pepper

Preheat oven to 350°F. Place each half of squash flesh side up on baking sheet. Mix together butter, honey, sugar, cinnamon, and lemon zest and juice; pour one-half of butter mixture on top of each squash half. Bake until very soft, approximately 1 to 1 1/2 hours. Remove from oven and cool. (This step can be done a day ahead.) Scoop out pulp of squash into bowl.

Place a medium-size stockpot over high heat. Add oil, onion, and celery; sauté until translucent, approximately 12 to 15 minutes. Add squash pulp and carrots and sauté another 2 minutes. Deglaze stockpot with brandy, then add fish stock, salt, and pepper. Bring to a boil. Reduce heat and simmer 30 minutes. Pour broth through strainer into another pot and keep hot. Check seasonings.

Pear Chutney

Yield: 2 cups

- 1 tablespoon olive oil
- $\frac{1}{2}$ small thinly sliced red onion
- 2 tablespoons white wine
- 2 tablespoons honey
- 2 tablespoons brown sugar
- 2 peeled, cored, and thinly sliced pears
- 1 teaspoon kosher salt
- $\frac{1}{2}$ teaspoon white pepper
- $\frac{1}{2}$ seeded and finely diced jalapeño

Heat a small saucepan over medium-high heat. Add oil and onion and sauté 5 minutes. Reduce heat and cook slowly until onion slices are caramelized, 15 to 20 minutes. Deglaze with wine, then add honey, sugar, and pears. Cook 30 minutes until pears are soft. Add salt, pepper, and jalapeño. Cook another 2 minutes. Serve warm or at room temperature.

Char is so closely related to trout that it is also sometimes referred to as steelhead trout. It is higher in fat content than trout but lower than salmon, and more expensive than both. The flesh is light pink to red and very delicate, and it looks quite similar to salmon. It is now farm raised in Canada and Scandinavian countries. Because the fillets are so delicate, they can be difficult to grill; pan roasting is an easier method of cooking.

arCtIcCHaR

Prosciutto-Wrapped Bluenose with Gnocchi and Sun-Dried Tomato Whiz

Yield: 4 servings

Prosciutto is an Italian ham that has been salt-cured, dried, and aged.

- 4 **thin slices prosciutto**
- 1½ **pounds bluenose, cut into 4 equal pieces**
- **Kosher salt and white pepper**
- 2 **tablespoons olive oil**
- 2 **tablespoons minced garlic**
- 2 **tablespoons minced shallots**
- 3 **tablespoons minced thyme**
- 3 **tablespoons minced oregano**
- 3 **tablespoons minced parsley**

- ½ **cup chopped kalamata olives**
- ¼ **cup drained and rinsed capers**
- ¼ **cup finely diced red onion**
- ¼ **cup white wine**
- 1 **cup fish stock (p. 2)**
- ½ **cup Sun-Dried Tomato Whiz**
- ½ **bunch trimmed asparagus Gnocchi**
- 3 **tablespoons melted butter, plus 6 tablespoons diced (3/4 stick)**

Bring to a boil two pots of water, one to blanch asparagus, the other to cook Gnocchi. Meanwhile, lay slices of prosciutto out on work surface. Season fish lightly with salt and pepper. Place 1 piece of fish topside down, not skin side, in center of each slice of prosciutto. Wrap ends of prosciutto around fish. Heat 1 tablespoon oil in a large sauté pan. When hot, place fish topside down in pan. Let sear on one side about 2 minutes. Flip fish. Add garlic and shallots and let sauté 1 minute. Add 1 tablespoon each of thyme, oregano, and parsley. Then add olives, capers, and onion and cook until liquid evaporates from pan. Remove fish from pan and keep fish warm in oven.

Deglaze pan with wine, then add fish stock and Sun-Dried Tomato Whiz. Bring to a boil and let reduce by one fourth. Meanwhile, blanch asparagus, 3 to 4 minutes, until bright green and just tender. Season with remaining olive oil, plus salt and pepper. Place a little less than half the Gnocchi (15 to 18 per person) in the other pot of boiling water. When the dumplings rise to water's surface, they are done. Remove them from water with slotted spoon and toss with melted butter and season with salt, pepper, and remaining herbs. Add diced butter to the olive pan sauce; swirl pan to incorporate.

 TO PLATE: *Divide asparagus among four dinner plates, with ends in center of plate. Place Gnocchi to the right of asparagus ends. Place fish on top of asparagus ends. Pour pan sauce over Gnocchi and fish.*

Gnocchi

Yield: 160 pieces, 8 servings

These pasta-like potato dumplings are surprisingly easy to make. Bake the potatoes a day ahead. This recipe makes quite a few gnocchi; just freeze any leftovers you don't cook—they keep well. Gnocchi can go straight from the freezer to boiling water; toss with a little butter, herbs, and Parmesan cheese, and voilà!

- **3 large baked and peeled Idaho potatoes**
- **1 cup flour**
- **3 eggs**
- **1 tablespoon kosher salt**
- **1 teaspoon white pepper**

Cut potatoes into large pieces. Press pieces through a ricer onto a floured work surface. Make a well in center of potatoes. Add 1/2 cup of flour and the eggs. Flour your hands and start kneading until flour and eggs are incorporated in potato mixture. Add remaining flour as needed to form a soft, slightly sticky, uniform dough. Be sure not to overmix or the dough will get tough. Cut dough into 6 portions and roll portions into snakes, 1/2-inch in diameter. Cut 3/4-inch-long pieces and then roll them over the back of a fork to form gnocchi.

Sun-Dried Tomato Whiz

Yield: 1/2 cup

- $\frac{1}{2}$ **cup sun-dried tomatoes**
- **1 tablespoon roasted garlic, plus 2 tablespoons oil (p. 3)**
- **2 tablespoons chopped basil**

Cover tomatoes in hot water and steep until soft, approximately 10 to 15 minutes. Remove tomatoes from water and reserve liquid. Place tomatoes in blender with roasted garlic, oil, and basil. Puree until smooth. It may be necessary to add a little reserved sun-dried tomato steeping water to smooth out puree.

9

A relatively new fish to the U.S. market, and often mistaken for grouper, bluenose is caught off the coasts of New Zealand and southern Australia. It has firm white flesh with red streaks and is very moist when cooked correctly. The fish is meaty and easy to grill.

bLueNoSe

Blackened Catfish with Shrimp Étouffée, Roasted Pepper Grits, and Hush Puppies

Yield: 6 servings

   Kosher salt
$\frac{1}{2}$ **cup JAX Blackening Spice**
$\frac{1}{2}$ **cup olive oil**
6 **catfish fillets, 8 to 10 ounces each**
3 **ears husked corn**
1 **cup beurre blanc, optional (p. 1)**
6 **parsley sprigs**
6 **lemon wedges**

Clean and oil surface of gas or charcoal grill, then preheat. Bring a large pot of salted water to a boil. Mix together JAX Blackening Spice and oil. Coat the topside of each of the catfish fillets with this blackening slurry. Place the catfish blackened side down on a hot grill. Cook 3 to 4 minutes, flip, and cook another 3 to 4 minutes. While the fish is cooking, place the corn in boiling salted water. Cook 10 minutes, drain, and cut in half.

TO PLATE: *Ladle approximately 1/2 cup (4 ounces) of Shrimp Étouffée onto each plate. Place half ear of corn standing up in center back of plate. Place 2 Hush Puppies to the left and 2 pieces of Roasted Pepper Grits in front of corn. Place catfish on top of grits. Pour beurre blanc over catfish and corn. Garnish with parsley sprigs and lemon wedges.*

This firm-textured bottom dweller is another farm-raised fish. You won't find any wild catfish unless you go and catch them yourself. Most farms are in Mississippi, where the conditions are optimal, but they are also springing up in Texas and Louisiana. The channel catfish is the species most farm raised. The saltwater variety of catfish is called hogfish. Farm-raised catfish are fed veggie pellets that float on the surface of the water, which has eliminated the muddy flavor that used to be associated with catfish. Traditionally, catfish has been breaded in cornmeal and fried, but it is also great blackened and grilled.

cAtFiSh

Catfish (Blackened Catfish plate continued from prior page...)

Shrimp Étouffée

Yield: 4 1/2 cups

$\frac{1}{2}$ pound (31–40 ct) shrimp, shells left on and deveined, plus 1/2 pound peeled and deveined

2 tablespoons olive oil

1 bottle or can (12 ounces) of your favorite beer (maybe it should be 2...1 for the étouffée and 1 for you!)

$\frac{1}{2}$ cup diced red pepper

$\frac{1}{2}$ cup diced green pepper

$\frac{1}{2}$ cup diced celery

$\frac{1}{2}$ cup diced onion

1 bay leaf

1 teaspoon dried thyme

1 teaspoon dried oregano

$\frac{1}{2}$ teaspoon chili flakes

$\frac{1}{8}$ teaspoon cayenne

$\frac{1}{2}$ teaspoon kosher salt

$\frac{1}{2}$ teaspoon black pepper

3 tablespoons toasted flour (p. 3)

3 tablespoons tomato paste

1 can (14.5 ounces) diced tomatoes

2 cups fish stock (p. 2)

TO DEVEIN SHRIMP: Without removing the shell, just snip the back of the shrimp with kitchen shears and remove vein.

TO MAKE SHRIMP STOCK: Heat a small saucepan over medium-high heat with 1 tablespoon of oil. Add shrimp with shells on. Sear shrimp until they turn pink. Deglaze with beer, then bring to a boil. Reduce heat and simmer 10 minutes. Remove from heat and let cool completely. Place shrimp and liquid in blender. Puree until smooth. Pour liquid through chinois or fine mesh strainer. This is your shrimp stock; you should have 1 cup. Set aside.

TO MAKE ÉTOUFFÉE: Heat remaining tablespoon of oil in a large stockpot over medium-high heat. Add red and green peppers, celery, and onion. Sauté until translucent, 10 to 12 minutes, stirring frequently; reduce heat as necessary. Add bay leaf, thyme, oregano, chili flakes, cayenne, salt, black pepper, and flour. Cook 5 minutes, until spices are toasted and flour covers all vegetables evenly. Stir frequently and reduce heat as necessary. Add tomato paste. Sauté another 5 minutes until tomato paste starts to caramelize. Stir frequently and reduce heat as necessary. Increase heat back to high. Deglaze with canned tomatoes, then add reserved shrimp stock and fish stock. Bring to a boil, reduce heat, and simmer for 30 minutes. The étouffée should become slightly thickened and almost gravy-like in consistency. Ten minutes before serving, add the peeled shrimp. Simmer until shrimp are cooked through.

12

Roasted Pepper Grits

Yield: 16 triangles, 8 servings

Be sure to cook grits until all of the water is absorbed before you bake them in the oven; this will ensure a really firm texture. It is better to make them a day ahead. These grits don't have to be fried. You can grill them or just reheat them in the oven.

- 4 tablespoons (1/2 stick) butter
- $\frac{1}{2}$ cup finely diced red onion
- $\frac{1}{2}$ cup chopped green onions
- 2 tablespoons minced garlic
- 2 teaspoons kosher salt
- 1 teaspoon white pepper
- 1 tablespoon minced thyme
- 1 tablespoon minced oregano
- 1 tablespoon minced parsley
- $\frac{1}{2}$ cup roasted and diced red pepper
- $\frac{1}{2}$ cup roasted and diced green pepper
- 4 cups fish stock (p. 2)
- 2 cups quick cooking grits
- $\frac{1}{2}$ cup grated Asiago cheese
- 2 tablespoons olive oil

Preheat oven to 350°F. Melt butter in an oven-safe, medium saucepan over medium-high heat. Add onions and garlic; sauté until garlic is fragrant, 2 to 3 minutes. Add salt, white pepper, herbs, roasted peppers, and fish stock. Bring to a boil and reduce heat to simmer. Whisk grits slowly into simmering liquid in a thin stream. Let cook 2 to 3 minutes until grits absorb all the liquid and thicken substantially. Stir in cheese. Cover loosely with foil and bake 30 minutes. Remove from oven and pour into a 13 x 9 x 2-inch baking dish and smooth to an even thickness. Place in the refrigerator to cool. When cooled completely, cut into 8 squares, then cut squares in half on a diagonal.

Heat oil in sauté pan over medium-high heat. Place the triangles in pan and fry for 2 to 3 minutes per side. You may have to do several batches. Don't crowd the pan with more than a few triangles at a time, as overcrowding the pan will cause grits to become mushy instead of crispy on the outside.

TO ROAST PEPPERS:
Place peppers on baking sheet and set under broiler. Let blister on all sides. When peppers are blistered all over, remove from oven and place in a paper or plastic bag to steam. When cool, remove blackened skin and seeds from peppers.

Hush Puppies

Yield: 24 hush puppies, 8 servings

- Oil for frying
- 1 cup sugar
- $1\frac{1}{2}$ cups cornmeal
- $1\frac{1}{2}$ cups flour
- 2 teaspoons baking powder
- 1 teaspoon baking soda
- 2 eggs
- 1 cup buttermilk
- 3 ounces (3/4 stick) melted butter

Preheat fryer to 375°F. Combine 1/2 cup sugar, cornmeal, flour, baking powder, and soda in a large mixing bowl and stir. Whisk together eggs and buttermilk in a small mixing bowl. Pour wet ingredients into dry; whisk together briefly. Whisk in melted butter. Let rest 1 hour. Batter will rise slightly, so make sure your bowl is large enough that it won't overflow. With a small ice cream scoop or two teaspoons, drop balls of dough into fryer and cook until crisp and golden brown, 8 to 10 minutes. Drain briefly on paper towels. Put remaining 1/2 cup sugar in a small bowl. Place warm Hush Puppies in bowl and roll around to coat with sugar.

13

Fried Calamari with Mango Chili Mojo

Yield: 2 1/4 cups sauce, 4 servings of calamari

Mojo, pronounced mo-ho, is the "salsa" of Cuba. It is a type of cooked vinaigrette, where garlic and spices are sautéed in oil and then an acid is added. Try to find fresh, very finely ground bread crumbs. The fresher and finer they are, the better they will stick to the calamari. If you are having trouble, just put bread crumbs in your food processor and grind a little more.

1	peeled and diced mango
$\frac{1}{3}$	cup water
1	cup sugar
$\frac{3}{4}$	cup rice wine vinegar
1	tablespoon olive oil
$\frac{1}{3}$	cup minced garlic
2	tablespoons chili flakes
	Oil for frying
1	pound cleaned calamari
2	cups fresh bread crumbs
	Kosher salt
	White pepper

TO MAKE MANGO CHILI MOJO: Place diced mango in blender. Add water and puree until smooth. Whisk together mango puree, sugar, and vinegar. Heat oil in a small saucepan and add garlic and chili flakes; sauté briefly 2 minutes. Whisk in mango puree and bring to a boil. Reduce heat and simmer 5 minutes.

TO COOK CALAMARI: Preheat fryer to 375ºF. Place calamari in a strainer to remove excess liquid. Place bread crumbs in a bowl. Add calamari and toss to coat evenly. Fry calamari 3 minutes, being careful not to overcook or it will become rubbery. Season with salt and pepper.

14

 TO PLATE: *Place Fried Calamari on a large platter with a ramekin or small bowl of room-temperature Mojo.*

There are three species of this cephalopod, the California (also called Pacific), the Atlantic longfin, and the Atlantic shortfin. Calamari is the most cost-effective seafood to use because it is 80 percent edible. You only need to remove the ink sac and internal plasticlike shell (known as cuttlebone, pen, or quill), slice up or stuff the body, and you are done. Cooking time is the most important aspect of calamari; if it is overcooked, it gets tough and rubbery, so make sure your pan or fryer is hot—cook for two to three minutes and eat immediately!

CaLaMaRi

CaViaR

It's not just from Russia anymore! Caviar is seeing a resurgence in popularity. It has been said that sturgeon can live between one hundred and two hundred years and grow to the enormous size of twenty-five hundred pounds. Due to industrialization around the Caspian Sea, they now live for about eighteen to thirty years and grow to between eighty and 150 pounds. Only sturgeon eggs from the Caspian Sea can be labeled as true caviar, which comes from the Turkish word havyar, meaning "egg." The Caspian Sea is also bordered by Iran and Kazakhstan. There are only two caviar harvests a year, one in spring and one in fall. All caviar must be processed through the Convention on International Trade in Endangered Species. So rest assured—sturgeon are not going to become extinct.

Most caviar purchased in the United States comes from three regions: Russia, the United States, and the Pacific Rim.

RUSSIAN STURGEON FROM THE CASPIAN SEA AND VOLGA RIVER

Beluga—the largest sturgeon, produces a large, black berry (egg); it is considered the best (and is the costliest).

Osetra—golden brown to gray in color, smaller berry than beluga, almost nutty flavor.

Sevruga—smallest berries, light gray, strongest flavor, most abundant, and consequently the least expensive.

AMERICAN CAVIARS FROM VARIOUS WATER SYSTEMS

American caviar is generally a little saltier than Russian or Iranian. Sturgeon were prevalent in American waters in the 1800s but were overfished and virtually extinct by 1900. They are being found again in the Great Lakes, the Mississippi River system, and in rivers and lakes of California. Many other types of fish are being explored for their caviars as well, with great success.

Paddlefish (spoonbill) sturgeon—small pearl gray berries, firm texture, found in the river systems of Tennessee, Alabama, Missouri, and Mississippi.

Hackleback sturgeon—small black egg, native to the waters of North America.

Salmon—large translucent red egg, found all over the United States.

Trout—small translucent red egg, also found all over the country.

Whitefish—yellow in color, small egg, present in the region of the Great Lakes.

Bowfin, dogfish, or choupique—shiny firm black egg, found in Louisiana.

PACIFIC RIM CAVIARS

Flying fish—from Japan; originally red to orange in color, very small berries, sometimes colored with wasabi powder for green eggs (no ham!).

Masago—smelt roe caviar from China.

Caviar

Yield: 2 servings

The word *molassol* on the label does not describe the type of caviar but rather that the roe is preserved with a minimum amount of salt (*molassol* is Russian for "little salt"). Store refrigerated in tightly sealed glass containers and use within a few days of opening jar. Metal should not come in contact with caviar, and the serving spoon should be made out of porcelain or carved from horn—metal can react with the eggs, causing a change in flavor.

1	jar (1 ounce) caviar
	Crushed ice
3	slices toasted bread, crusts removed
1	hard-boiled egg
$\frac{1}{4}$	cup brunoise red onion
2	tablespoons capers
1	lemon, cut into wedges
$\frac{1}{4}$	cup of your favorite olives

Place caviar jar in crushed ice in a small bowl or caviar server. Cut toasted bread into quarters and then diagonally to form triangles. Separate egg yolk and white. Press each separately through a fine mesh strainer.

 TO PLATE: *Arrange strained egg yolk, egg white, onion, and capers in straight lines on a platter surrounded with toast points. Serve with iced caviar. Garnish with lemons and olives.*

Pan-Roasted Chilean Sea Bass with Beluga Lentils and Roasted Butternut

Yield: 8 servings

Beluga lentils are named for their color. Like beluga caviar, they are small and black. If you cannot find black lentils, substitute green.

3	tablespoons olive oil
2	tablespoons minced garlic
2	tablespoons minced shallots
3	tablespoons minced thyme
3	tablespoons minced oregano
2	cups beluga lentils
4	cups fish stock (p. 2)
1	bunch trimmed asparagus
	Kosher salt and white pepper
3	pounds Chilean sea bass, cut into 8 portions
1	bunch minced parsley
2	tablespoons flour
1	cup beurre blanc (p. 1)

Preheat oven to 400°F. Heat 1 tablespoon of oil in small stockpot. Add garlic, shallots, thyme, and oregano. Sauté until fragrant, 2 to 3 minutes. Add lentils and fish stock. Bring to a boil. Reduce heat and simmer until lentils are al dente, about 45 minutes. Keep stirring and checking the lentils—you may have to add a little water. Lentils overcook quickly and easily, so turn off the heat just before they are done. They will continue cooking until cool.

Coat asparagus in 1 tablespoon of oil and season with salt and pepper. Place asparagus on a baking sheet and roast in the oven until tender, about 15 minutes. Heat the remaining tablespoon of oil in a sauté pan large enough to hold the sea bass without crowding. Season fish with 2 tablespoons of the minced parsley, salt, and pepper. Dust lightly with flour. When pan and oil are very hot, add fish and sear on one side, 2 to 3 minutes. Turn over and finish roasting in oven, about 5 minutes.

 TO PLATE: *Ladle 1/2 cup (4 ounces) of Roasted Butternut Squash Bisque onto each plate and tilt plate to cover entire base. Place large scoop of beluga lentils in the center of each plate. Divide asparagus among plates and arrange with tips toward outer edge of plate, in a star shape, with bases together in the center of the plate. Place fish on top of asparagus bases. Drizzle with beurre blanc and garnish with minced parsley.*

Caught only in the Antarctic waters of the Southern Hemisphere, this fish is not really a bass at all but is more aptly named Patagonian toothfish. They can grow to one hundred pounds and were thought to have been overfished a couple of years ago. Chilean sea bass swim in very deep waters of up to one thousand feet, so it is very hard to say for certain if they are dwindling in numbers. They begin spawning at ten to twelve years and can live up to fifty years. Recently, they have been caught off other coasts such as Peru, which indicates there may be other populations of this fish yet to be discovered. It is a fairly oily fish, with a firm texture, full flavor, and white flesh, very moist. Chilean sea bass has a tendency to flake apart when cooking, so it is better to pan roast than grill.

Roasted Butternut Squash Bisque

Yield: 8 cups

You may want to make this sauce a day ahead so it can cool before pureeing and straining.

1	halved and seeded butternut squash	1	teaspoon dried thyme
2	cloves peeled garlic, plus 1 tablespoon minced	1	teaspoon dried oregano
5	tablespoons butter	$\frac{1}{8}$	teaspoon allspice
$1\frac{1}{2}$	teaspoons kosher salt, plus more for seasoning	$\frac{1}{8}$	teaspoon nutmeg
$\frac{3}{4}$	teaspoon black pepper, plus more for seasoning	1	bay leaf
1	tablespoon olive oil	8	tablespoons flour
$\frac{1}{2}$	pound (31–40 ct) shrimp, shells left on	$\frac{1}{4}$	cup white wine
1	diced small onion	3	cups fish stock (p. 2)
2	tablespoons minced shallots	1	cup heavy cream
1	peeled and chopped carrot	$\frac{1}{4}$	cup brandy
2	tablespoons tomato paste		

19

Preheat oven to 350°F. Place squash halves cut side up on a baking sheet and top with garlic cloves, 1 tablespoon of butter, 1/2 teaspoon of salt, and 1/4 teaspoon of pepper. Place in oven and roast until tender, approximately 1 hour. Scoop pulp from skin and set aside. In a large pot, add oil and shrimp (with shells on) and sauté about 3 to 4 minutes until shrimp turn pink. Add onion, minced garlic, and shallots. Cook another 5 minutes until diced onion is tender. Add squash pulp, carrot, tomato paste, thyme, oregano, the remaining 1 teaspoon salt and 1/2 teaspoon pepper, plus allspice, nutmeg, and bay leaf. Reduce heat as necessary to avoid burning. Cook, stirring frequently, another 12 to 15 minutes, toasting spices and caramelizing tomato paste.

Add remaining 4 tablespoons butter to pot and let melt; add flour and stir to coat vegetables. Cook 8 minutes, stirring frequently. Increase heat back to high. Deglaze with white wine, then add fish stock, cream, and brandy. Bring to a boil. Reduce heat and simmer 20 minutes. Remove from heat and cool completely. Puree in small batches in blender and strain through fine mesh sieve. Bring back to a boil. Season with salt and pepper.

SeA BaSs

Before using clams, scrub their shells to remove any grit and make sure that all the shells are tightly closed. It is best to use clams immediately, but if you cannot, just keep them cold—and let them breath in a bowl in the fridge, with a damp cloth on top. Don't immerse them in water. Most clams are served steamed, but they are also great grilled, baked, or fried.

cLAmS

Manila clams—These delicate beauties were accidentally introduced from Japan in the 1930s, with some Japanese oyster seeds to Washington State bays, similar to littlenecks, but smaller and sweeter.

New Zealand cockles—Similar to clams but not in the same family, New Zealand cockles are smaller, with white shells that have green stripes. They are sweet and have very tender meat.

Soft-shell clams—Steamers, longnecks, and geoducks are in this category. Soft-shell clams are characterized by their oval-shaped shells and protruding necks; the shells are more delicate but definitely not soft. These clams are much more prevalent on the East Coast.

Hard-shell clams—Quahog, cherrystone, littleneck, and topnecks are in this category. Generally speaking, the larger the clam the tougher and chewier. Hard-shell clams are generally classified by size.

Manhattan Clam Chowda

Yield: 8 cups

This is a great first course for eight, or serve it with a salad and some sourdough bread as an entrée for four. Be sure to add the chopped clams at the last minute or they will be rubbery!

2 **tablespoons olive oil**
1 **tablespoon minced garlic**
1 **tablespoon minced shallots**
1 **tablespoon minced thyme**
1 **tablespoon minced oregano**
2 **pounds Manila clams**
$\frac{1}{2}$ **cup white wine**
1 **cup water**
1 **cup diced onion**
1 **cup diced celery**
1 **cup peeled and diced carrots**
2 **cups tomato juice**
1 **can (14.5 ounces) diced tomatoes**
3 **cups diced Yukon gold potatoes**
$\frac{1}{8}$ **teaspoon paprika**
   Pinch cayenne
1 **teaspoon Worcestershire sauce**
1 **teaspoon Cholula**
$\frac{1}{2}$ **teaspoon kosher salt**
$\frac{1}{4}$ **teaspoon white pepper**

Heat 1 tablespoon of oil in a pan large enough to hold and cover the clams. Add garlic and shallots and sauté 2 minutes until fragrant. Add thyme, oregano, and clams, then deglaze with wine and add water. Cover and bring to a boil. Reduce heat slightly and cook until all clams are wide open. Remove clams from broth (reserve broth—you should have 1 1/2 cups) and let clams cool. Remove meat from shells and coarsely chop; set aside.

In a large pot, heat remaining tablespoon of oil. Add onion, celery, and carrots and sauté about 10 minutes, until tender. Deglaze with reserved clam broth. Add remaining ingredients and bring to a boil. Reduce heat and simmer until potatoes are tender.

 TO PLATE: *Ladle soup into bowls and garnish with chopped clam meat.*

New England Clam Chowda

Yield: 8 cups

This makes eight appetizers or a hearty meal for four with a green salad and some crusty bread.

1 tablespoon olive oil	1 cup finely diced celery
2 tablespoons minced garlic	1 cup julienne leeks
2 tablespoons minced shallots	2 tablespoons butter
1 tablespoon minced thyme	2 tablespoons flour
1 tablespoon minced oregano	2 cups cooked and diced red potatoes
2 pounds Manila clams	2 cups heavy cream
1 cup white wine	1 tablespoon kosher salt
3 cups water	1 teaspoon black pepper
$\frac{1}{4}$ cup finely diced bacon	Freshly ground black pepper
1 cup finely diced onion	Minced parsley for garnish

Heat oil in a saucepot large enough to hold and cover the clams. Add garlic, shallots, thyme, oregano, and clams to pot. Cook over medium-high heat for 3 to 4 minutes, until garlic becomes fragrant and liquid evaporates. Deglaze with 1/2 cup wine, then add water. Cover and cook 5 to 6 minutes until all clams are open. Cool. Reserve cooking liquid (you should have 3 cups) and remove clam meat from shells. Chop clam meat and set aside.

Heat bacon in a medium stockpot and cook until crispy and rendered. Add onion, celery, and leeks. Sauté vegetables until all liquid is released and vegetables begin to caramelize slightly, 10 to 12 minutes. Add butter and let melt. Add flour; stir to coat vegetables. Toast flour, stirring frequently to avoid burning, 5 to 8 minutes. Deglaze with remaining 1/2 cup of wine. Add potatoes, reserved clam stock, cream, salt, and pepper. Bring to a boil. Reduce heat to low and simmer 30 minutes.

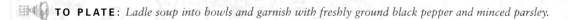 **TO PLATE:** *Ladle soup into bowls and garnish with freshly ground black pepper and minced parsley.*

Clam Po'Boy with Rémoulade and JAX Slaw with Honey Fennel Vinaigrette

Yield: 12 servings

Oil for fryer	Kosher salt and white pepper
12 ears corn	1 head chiffonade romaine lettuce
5 pounds new potatoes	8 sliced Roma tomatoes
3 baguettes	1 cup beurre blanc (p. 1)
2 cups flour	1 batch Hush Puppies (p. 13)
4 beaten eggs	Mayonnaise, optional
4 cups fresh bread crumbs	Pickle relish, optional
3 pounds drained clam strips	

Preheat fryer to 375°F. Place two large pots of water over high heat. When they start to boil, cook the corn in one for 8 minutes and potatoes in the other until tender, 10 to 12 minutes. Turn off heat just before done and let sit in water to keep warm until serving. Cut each baguette into 4 sections. Cut each section in half lengthwise and hollow it out slightly. Place flour, eggs, and bread crumbs in three small separate bowls. Place clams in bowl with flour; toss to coat. Remove clams, shake off excess flour, and place clams in egg wash; stir to coat. Place clams in bowl with bread crumbs; toss to coat. Place breaded clams in fryer and cook just until browned and crispy, 3 to 5 minutes. Do several batches. Don't overcook or clams will become rubbery. Season with salt and pepper.

  TO PLATE: *Place a mound of JAX Slaw with Honey Fennel Vinaigrette on each plate. Lean baguettes on slaw and fill with romaine and Roma tomatoes. Divide fried clams between po'boy "buns." Top clams with a heaping tablespoon of Rémoulade. Top slaw with a dollop of mayo and relish. Serve po'boys with bowls of smoking hot corn, steamed potatoes that have been drizzled in beurre blanc, and Hush Puppies.*

Rémoulade

Yield: 3 cups

This is a great spread for any sandwich.

1 cup whole-grain mustard	1 teaspoon celery seed
$\frac{1}{2}$ cup horseradish	1 teaspoon kosher salt
$\frac{1}{2}$ cup white wine vinegar	1 teaspoon black pepper
2 tablespoons paprika	$\frac{1}{2}$ cup minced parsley
$\frac{1}{2}$ tablespoon Chimayo chili powder	1 cup mayonnaise
1 bunch minced green onions	

Place all ingredients in a large bowl and whisk thoroughly to remove any paprika clumps. Refrigerate until ready to use.

JAX Slaw with Honey Fennel Vinaigrette

Yield: 2 1/4 cups vinaigrette, 12 servings of slaw

Dress the slaw just before serving so it stays crisp. The dressing is great on other salads, too.

1 head thinly sliced green cabbage	$\frac{1}{2}$ cup rice wine vinegar	1 tablespoon ground fennel seeds
$\frac{1}{2}$ head thinly sliced red cabbage	$\frac{1}{2}$ cup cider vinegar	$\frac{1}{2}$ teaspoon kosher salt
3 peeled and grated carrots	$\frac{1}{4}$ cup honey	$\frac{1}{2}$ teaspoon black pepper
	$\frac{1}{4}$ cup sugar	1 cup olive oil

Place cabbage and carrots in large bowl and toss together thoroughly.

TO MAKE HONEY FENNEL VINAIGRETTE: In a large bowl, whisk together rice wine vinegar, cider vinegar, honey, sugar, fennel seeds, salt, and pepper until honey and sugar dissolve. Whisk in oil. Dress slaw according to taste.

23

Manila Clams with Grilled Corn, New Potatoes, and Shallot Compound Butter

Yield: 2 servings

- **2   ears cooked corn**
- **2   strips minced applewood-smoked bacon**
- **2   pounds rinsed and scrubbed Manila clams**
- **6   diced baby red potatoes**
- **1   cup fish stock (p. 2)**

TO PLATE:
Divide into two bowls and serve with bread to soak up the yummy sauce.

Clean and oil surface of charcoal or gas grill, then pre-heat. Set corn on grill surface and char slightly. Let cool and cut into 1-inch-thick wheels. Place bacon in a stockpot over high heat, and render until crispy. Add clams, corn, and potatoes. Cook 2 minutes, then deglaze with fish stock. Cover clams and cook 3 to 4 minutes until opened. Add two 1/2-inch-thick slices of Shallot Compound Butter and swirl pan to melt.

24

Shallot Compound Butter

Yield: 3/4 cup

Butter will keep frozen in an airtight container for up to one month.

- **$\frac{1}{4}$ pound (1 stick) softened butter**
- **$\frac{1}{4}$ cup minced shallots**
- **1   teaspoon JAX Old Bay Seafood Seasoning**
- **1   teaspoon black pepper**
- **1   teaspoon lemon juice**

Whip all ingredients together in a food processor or standing mixer. Scrape onto a sheet of parchment or waxed paper, approximately 8 1/2 x 11 inches. Fold paper in half over butter mixture and press into a cylinder shape. Roll paper around butter cylinder and twist ends to seal. Place in freezer for 1 hour. Remove from freezer and cut 1/2-inch-thick slices to serve.

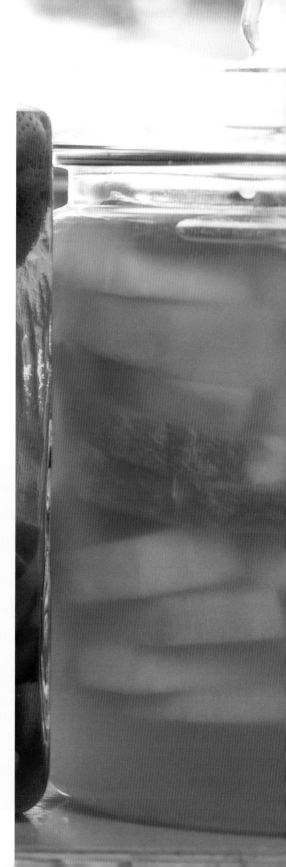

cOcKtAiLs

Because the bar is such a fun part of JAX, here are some of our most famous concoctions.

Bahama Mama

Yield: 1 cocktail

> Ice
> 1 ounce light rum
> 1 ounce dark rum
> ½ ounce vodka
> ½ ounce sweet and sour mix
> 1 ounce orange juice
> 3 ounces pineapple juice
> Dash grenadine
> 1 orange slice
> 1 lime slice
> 1 maraschino cherry

Fill 1 (14-ounce) glass with ice. Add both rums, vodka, sweet and sour mix, orange juice, pineapple juice, and grenadine. Shake and garnish with a slice of orange and lime and a maraschino cherry.

Twistini

Yield: 1 martini

> Ice
> 3 ounces vodka
> ½ ounce freshly squeezed lime juice
> ½ ounce raspberry liqueur
> 1 big lemon twist

Fill martini shaker with ice. Add vodka, lime juice, and raspberry liquor. Shake well. Strain into a martini glass and serve with a lemon twist tied in a knot.

Melondrama

Yield: 1 cocktail

> Ice
> 1 ounce Midori liqueur
> 1 ounce vodka
> 3 ounces apple juice
> 1½ ounces sweet and sour mix
> ½ ounce freshly squeezed lime juice
> 1 cantaloupe ball
> 1 honeydew melon ball
> 1 watermelon ball

Fill a 14-ounce glass with ice. Add Midori, vodka, apple juice, sweet and sour mix, and lime juice. Shake and serve garnished with a spear of a cantaloupe, honeydew, and watermelon balls.

Oyster Shooter

Yield: 1 cocktail

- **1 ounce Five-Pepper Infused Vodka**
- **2 ounces JAX Bloody Mary Mix**
- **1 freshly shucked oyster**
- **1 lemon wedge**

Place all ingredients and a squeeze of lemon in a martini glass. Bottoms up!

Spicy Shrimp Bloody Mary

Yield: 1 cocktail

- **Ice**
- **2 ounces Five-Pepper Infused Vodka**
- **5 ounces JAX Bloody Mary Mix**
- **3 cooked, peeled, and deveined small (31–40 ct) shrimp**
- **1 peperoncini**
- **1 jalapeño-stuffed olive**
- **1 lime wedge**

Fill 1 (14-ounce) glass with ice. Add vodka and JAX Bloody Mary Mix. Garnish with the shrimp hanging off rim of glass and the peperoncini, olive, and lime wedge in the drink. Serve and enjoy.

JAX
Bloody Mary Mix
Yield: 2 liters

1 tablespoon Cholula
2 tablespoons Worcestershire sauce
2 tablespoons black pepper
1 tablespoon celery seed
1 tablespoon celery salt
$\frac{1}{2}$ cup horseradish
1 teaspoon kosher salt
2 tablespoons lemon juice
2 tablespoons lime juice
1 can (46 ounces) tomato juice

Mix all ingredients except tomato juice in large bowl or pitcher. Add tomato juice and blend completely.

Five-Pepper
Infused Vodka
Yield: 2 liters

1 Anaheim chili pepper
1 serrano chili pepper
1 poblano pepper
1 ancho pepper
1 jalapeño
2 (1-liter) bottles vodka

Place all ingredients in a large glass or plastic container and let marinate in a cool place for 2 days.

27

Fried Corvina with Mustard Greens, Molasses BBQ Sauce, Baked White Beans, an

Yield: 6 servings

You can substitute shrimp if corvina is not available.

Oil for frying

3 cups JAX rice (p. 2)

2 eggs

1 cup your favorite beer

1 cup flour

1 tablespoon olive oil

1 tablespoon minced garlic

1 tablespoon minced shallots

3 cups washed and chopped mustard green leaves

$\frac{1}{2}$ tablespoon lemon juice

Kosher salt and white pepper

3 pounds corvina, cut into 1-inch-wide strips

Preheat fryer to 375°F. Make JAX rice and keep warm. In a small bowl, whisk together eggs, beer, and flour; set aside. Place a large sauté pan over medium-high heat. Add oil, garlic, and shallots and cook 2 to 3 minutes. Add mustard greens and cook 2 to 4 minutes, until wilted. Deglaze with lemon juice, then season with salt and pepper. Turn off heat. Dip corvina in beer batter and slowly drop into fryer. Let fish fry 3 to 5 minutes, depending on thickness of fillet. You will have to do several batches depending on the size of your fryer. Season with salt and pepper to taste.

 TO PLATE: *Place a large spoonful of rice in center of each plate. Add a large spoonful of Baked White Beans to the right and a few mustard greens to the left. In front center of plates, ladle 1/4 cup (2 ounces) of Molasses BBQ Sauce. Place 3 to 4 strips of corvina on top of sauce and Red Onion Jam on top of fish.*

Molasses BBQ Sauce

Yield: 3 cups

3 shallots

5 Roma tomatoes

2 tablespoons olive oil

3 tablespoons roasted garlic (p. 3)

3 tablespoons bourbon

$\frac{1}{4}$ cup molasses

$\frac{1}{2}$ teaspoon kosher salt

$\frac{1}{2}$ teaspoon black pepper

$\frac{1}{4}$ teaspoon chili flakes

$\frac{1}{2}$ teaspoon mustard powder

1 tablespoon Worcestershire sauce

1 cup ketchup

1 can (14.5 ounces) diced tomatoes

Preheat oven to 375°F. Toss shallots and tomatoes with 1 tablespoon of the oil. Place shallots and tomatoes on baking sheet in oven for 60 to 90 minutes, until shallots have softened and blackened slightly and tomato skins have cracked. In a saucepan, combine remaining 1 tablespoon of oil, roasted shallots and tomatoes, and roasted garlic. Cook over medium-high heat for 12 to 15 minutes, until shallots, tomatoes, and garlic cook down and blend together. Add remaining ingredients. Bring to a boil. Reduce heat and simmer 30 minutes. Cool completely. Puree in blender and strain through mesh sieve. Reheat sauce and check seasonings.

Also sometimes sold/marketed as bass, corvina is a small fish caught far off the coast of Portugal. The tender, flaky white meat is sold in fillets. Because it is so small and flaky, pan roasting is recommended over grilling.

cOrViNa

Baked White Beans
Yield: 8 cups

3 finely diced applewood-smoked bacon strips

4 cups fish stock (p. 3)

1 smoked and diced red onion

2 cups uncooked white beans, soaked overnight in water

6 sprigs thyme

3 tablespoons whole-grain mustard

$\frac{1}{4}$ cup brown sugar

$\frac{1}{4}$ cup molasses

$\frac{1}{2}$ tablespoon black pepper

2 tablespoons minced parsley

$\frac{1}{2}$ tablespoon kosher salt

Place bacon in a stockpot over high heat and render until crispy. Add fish stock, onion, and drained beans. Bring to a boil. Reduce heat and simmer until beans are tender—about 2 hours. You may have to add water. Preheat oven to 350°F. Remove beans from heat and place in roasting pan. Add remaining ingredients and cover with water. Bake for 1 hour, until liquid reduces to a gravy-like consistency.

Red Onion Jam
Yield: 1 cup

1 tablespoon olive oil

4 thinly sliced red onions

1 cup port wine

$\frac{1}{4}$ cup brown sugar

2 tablespoons minced thyme

29

Place oil in large, heavy-bottom sauté pan over high heat. Add onions and let cook on high heat for 5 to 8 minutes, until onions are tender and start to caramelize. Reduce heat to medium and continue to sweat onions, stirring frequently. Continue to reduce heat by small increments to caramelize onions completely without burning them. This process will take approximately 30 to 45 minutes. The onions will turn dark purple in color and will reduce to 1 cup. Deglaze with port, then add brown sugar and thyme. Let cook until liquid evaporates. Remove from heat.

TO SMOKE ONIONS: Line bottom of broiler pan with foil. Place 1/2 cup wood chips on foil. Peel and quarter onion. Place on top of perforated pan of broiler set. Cover the onion and pan with foil to keep the smoke contained. Place pan over gas flame either outside on a gas grill or over a gas range burner with hood. Chips must be placed directly over the flame. Chips will begin to smoke after 3 to 5 minutes. Keep heat on for another 3 minutes. Turn off heat and let onions continue to smoke for another 5 minutes. Carefully remove foil from top of pan to avoid a large face full of smoke, starting with the side furthest away from you. You may want to remove foil outside.

Fried Soft-Shell Crabs over Chuka Soba Noodle Stir-Fry with Sesame Ginger Vinaigrette

Yield: 6 servings

Oil for frying

1 **cup flour**

1 **teaspoon kosher salt, plus more for seasoning**

$\frac{1}{2}$ **teaspoon white pepper, plus more for seasoning**

$\frac{1}{4}$ **teaspoon cayenne**

2 **eggs, beaten with 1 tablespoon of water**

2 **cups fresh bread crumbs**

1 **tablespoon vegetable oil**

1 **tablespoon minced garlic**

2 **tablespoons minced gingerroot**

4 **cups sliced shiitake mushrooms**

1 **julienne red pepper**

2 **cups sugar snap peas**

6 **heads washed and chopped baby bok choy**

$\frac{1}{4}$ **cup Sesame Ginger Vinaigrette**

2 **tablespoons sesame oil**

1 **package (10 ounces) chuka soba noodles, cooked**

12 **cleaned soft-shell crabs**

Sweet soy sauce

Preheat fryer to 375°F. In a medium-size bowl, combine flour, 1 teaspoon salt, 1/2 teaspoon pepper, and cayenne. Place eggs and bread crumbs in two other separate bowls. Place vegetable oil in a large sauté pan over high heat. When hot, add garlic, ginger, and mushrooms and sauté for 2 to 3 minutes. Add red pepper, peas, and bok choy; cook another 2 minutes. Add 1/4 cup Sesame Ginger Vinaigrette and quickly toss to coat vegetables. Remove from heat.

In another sauté pan (nonstick), heat sesame oil over high heat. Add cooked noodles and stir-fry until they start to get crispy, 3 to 5 minutes. Dip the soft-shell crabs into seasoned flour, then eggs, and then bread crumbs. Slowly lower crabs into hot fryer oil. Cook 3 to 5 minutes, remove, and drain briefly on paper towels. Season with salt and pepper.

Sesame Ginger Vinaigrette
Yield: 1 1/2 cups

$\frac{1}{4}$ **cup pickled ginger**

$\frac{1}{4}$ **cup soy sauce**

$1\frac{1}{2}$ **teaspoons minced garlic**

$\frac{1}{4}$ **bunch minced cilantro**

$\frac{1}{4}$ **bunch minced green onions**

$1\frac{1}{2}$ **teaspoons wasabi powder**

$\frac{1}{4}$ **cup rice wine vinegar**

$\frac{1}{4}$ **teaspoon kosher salt**

$\frac{1}{8}$ **teaspoon white pepper**

2 **tablespoons sesame oil**

$\frac{1}{2}$ **cup vegetable oil**

Place all ingredients in blender except for oils and puree until smooth. With blender running, slowly incorporate oils.

 TO PLATE: *Place stir-fried noodles in center of individual serving plates. Arrange vegetables around noodles. Place 2 soft-shell crabs on top of noodles. Drizzle with sweet soy sauce.*

Blue crab—*Callinectes sepidus,* "beautiful swimmer," these crabs have flattened hind legs that enable them to swim. They are four to six inches in diameter and are caught as far north as the coast of Maryland, around the coast of Florida, and all the way around the Gulf of Mexico. Their shells are tinged with blue before cooking. The females have red-tipped claws and turn bright red after cooking. They can be found live in Asian markets, but most of the time you will find them cooked whole and sometimes frozen. They are abundant in summer and scarce in winter.

Dungeness—These crabs weigh three to four pounds and are native to the Pacific Coast, from Mexico to Alaska, and are sold whole, live, or cooked. Lucky for us, these crabs are abundant in winter—which is the opposite of blue crabs—and scarce in summer, so we can have good crab all year-round.

Snow crab—Snow crab is the more appealing marketing name for either tanner or spider crabs. They weigh three to four pounds and live six years. They are also caught off the north Pacific Coast and are prized for their long legs; they have a slightly softer shell than blue or Dungeness.

Soft-shell crab—These spring and summer delicacies are blue crabs that have molted their shells. They stay soft in the water for a couple of hours when they are caught and shipped live. Their shells cannot harden when out of the water. These crabs can stay alive for a couple of days out of water and that's the best way to get them. You can sometimes find them out of season in your grocer's freezer—but we don't recommend them.

Stone crab—It is illegal to catch a whole stone crab off the coast of Florida. Stone crabs are also found off the coasts of Texas and Mexico. These burrowing crabs are fished exclusively for their claws, but only one at a time. They are pulled from the water, one claw and arm are removed, and then they are thrown back to sea to regenerate another. Stone crabs are distinctive because of their very hard shells and black tips on the ends of their claws. Stone crab claws are only available cooked, from November to May.

King crab—These crabs are also prized for their legs. They can be found in the north Pacific Ocean and are also sometimes called Alaskan or Antarctic crabs. They are similar to snow crabs except much larger, sometimes reaching twenty-five pounds and six feet in diameter.

Rock crab—Also sometimes called Jonah crabs, they are named for their very hard shells. They are larger than blue crabs but smaller than Dungeness and are found all along the Atlantic coast.

31

TO CLEAN A SOFT-SHELL CRAB: Always try to get live soft-shell crabs; they are the best. With a sharp pair of kitchen shears, snip off the face of the crab. This kills the crab instantly. Next, flip it over and remove the apron—it looks like a wide flat tail that lays flat against the crab's belly. A wide apron represents a female crab, narrow a male. Now, lift the sides of the top shell and snip out the gills. Be sure to get all of them because they contain water that will splatter oil when frying.

Damn Good Crab Cakes with Red Pepper Louie

Yield: 10 cakes, 5 servings

Yes, they are damn good. Be sure to get the best-tasting crab available—Phillips, if you can find it.

1 tablespoon minced garlic	1 teaspoon chopped parsley, plus sprigs for garnish
$\frac{1}{4}$ cup diced onion	$\frac{1}{2}$ teaspoon Cholula
$\frac{1}{4}$ cup diced celery	$\frac{1}{2}$ teaspoon kosher salt
$\frac{1}{4}$ cup diced red pepper	$\frac{1}{2}$ teaspoon black pepper
$\frac{1}{4}$ cup diced green pepper	$1\frac{1}{2}$ cups fresh bread crumbs
1 tablespoon olive oil	1 egg
$\frac{1}{4}$ cup mayonnaise	1 pound backfin crabmeat
1 tablespoon Dijon mustard	$\frac{1}{2}$ cup clarified butter
1 teaspoon lemon zest, plus 5 wedges for garnish	

Place garlic, onion, celery, and red and green peppers in food processor. Pulse until finely chopped. Do not puree. Place oil in small sauté pan over medium-high heat, then add chopped vegetable mix. Sauté the vegetables until all liquid has evaporated from pan. Remove vegetable mix from pan and let cool completely. In a large bowl, combine mayonnaise, mustard, lemon zest, parsley, Cholula, salt, pepper, and cold vegetable mix. Blend thoroughly. Add bread crumbs and egg. Mix well. Gently fold in crabmeat. Divide meat into 10 equal-sized cakes.

Place 1 to 2 tablespoons of clarified butter in a large sauté pan or griddle over medium-high heat. Place cakes in sauté pan and let cakes cook 3 to 4 minutes. Flip cakes over and let cook another 3 to 4 minutes. You may have to do more than one batch to avoid overcrowding the sauté pan. Keep cakes warm in the oven while remaining cakes are cooking.

TO PLATE: *Place 2 cakes on small serving plate with Red Pepper Louie. Garnish with lemon wedge and parsley sprig.*

TO MAKE FRESH BREAD CRUMBS: Two ounces of stale bread should make approximately 1 cup of fresh bread crumbs. Place approximately 1 slice of stale bread in a blender or food processor. Process bread into fine, even-grained crumbs.

TO MAKE CLARIFIED BUTTER: Whole butter has a much lower smoking temperature (burning point) than clarified butter. To get that fabulous butter flavor, clarifying is necessary to remove the solids that burn at a lower temperature. Take 4 ounces (1 stick) butter and melt it in a small heavy-bottom saucepan over medium-high heat. Skim foam from top and then remove from heat; let butter solids separate from fat. The solids will sink to the bottom of the pan and the butterfat will rise to the top. Ladle or pour off the butterfat and discard the solids. Yields approximately 3 ounces, or 6 tablespoons.

32

Red Pepper Louie

Yield: 1 1/2 cups

Add more or less horseradish to increase or decrease the heat of this sauce, depending on your taste. Chili sauce is found in grocery stores in the condiment section.

- 1 **cup mayonnaise**
- 1 **tablespoon chili sauce**
- 1 **teaspoon Worcestershire sauce**
- 1 **tablespoon minced scallions**
- 1 **tablespoon fresh lemon juice**
- 1 **teaspoon brandy**
- 2 **tablespoons Atomic Horseradish**
- 1 **tablespoon finely diced red pepper**
- **Dash kosher salt and white pepper**

Combine all the ingredients in a large bowl. Whisk thoroughly until there are no lumps.

Crab and Smoked Tomato Gazpacho

Yield: 6 cups, 12 servings

- 5   smoked Roma tomatoes
- 1   small finely diced red pepper
- 1   small finely diced green pepper
- 1   seeded and finely diced jalapeño
- $\frac{1}{4}$ cup finely diced red onion
- 2   peeled, seeded, and finely diced cucumbers
- 1   zested and juiced lemon
- 2   zested and juiced limes
- 2   tablespoons minced parsley
- 2   tablespoons minced cilantro
- 2   cups tomato juice
- 2   tablespoons olive oil
- 1   tablespoon Cholula
- $\frac{1}{2}$ teaspoon kosher salt
- $\frac{1}{4}$ teaspoon white pepper
- $\frac{1}{2}$ cup crème fraîche (p. 2)
- $\frac{1}{2}$ pound crabmeat

34

Put tomatoes in a blender and puree. Strain through a mesh sieve and place tomato puree in a large bowl. Add red and green peppers, jalapeño, onion, cucumbers, lemon and lime juice and zest, parsley, and cilantro. Whisk to blend. Slowly stir in tomato juice until you get a soup consistency. Add olive oil, Cholula, and salt and pepper.

 TO PLATE: *Place crème fraîche in a squeeze tube. Ladle soup into bowls and drizzle with crème fraîche and garnish with crab.*

TO SMOKE THE TOMATOES: Soak 1/2 cup wood chips in water for 30 minutes. Clean and oil surface of gas or charcoal grill, then preheat. Place wet wood chips directly on hot charcoal; or if you are using a gas grill, place wet wood chips in a smoke box (a metal box with holes in the top to let the smoke escape) directly on top of the gas flame, which means under the cooking surface. Place tomatoes on the grill. The wood chips should ignite and start smoking within a few minutes. Cover grill and let tomatoes smoke for approximately 5 minutes. Open grill, turn tomatoes over, and let smoke another 5 minutes.

CrAw

Also known as crayfish, crawdads, mudbugs, or a plethora of other names, crawfish look like tiny freshwater lobsters. They average three and a half inches long and are sold live or cooked, fresh or frozen. They are farm raised in rice fields, alternating seasons with rice crops. There are 350 species of crawfish worldwide. Most are farm raised in Louisiana and can grow to be nine inches long. The most common farm-raised species in the United States is the red swamp crawfish.

FiSh

Brunswick Stew

Yield: 2 servings

We substituted baby lima beans for traditional favas in this one.

- 1 tablespoon olive oil
- 2 tablespoons minced garlic
- 2 tablespoons minced shallots
- 6 whole crawfish
- $\frac{1}{2}$ cup crawfish tails
- 1 cup baby lima beans
- $\frac{1}{2}$ cup chopped, blanched asparagus
- 1 tablespoon minced oregano
- 1 tablespoon minced thyme
- $\frac{1}{4}$ teaspoon kosher salt
- $\frac{1}{2}$ teaspoon white pepper
- 3 tablespoons butter
- 4 tablespoons toasted flour (p. 3)
- $\frac{1}{2}$ cup peeled and deveined small (31–40 ct) shrimp
- 2 cups fish stock (p. 2)
- 2 ounces julienne strips of Virginia ham

Place oil in a large sauté pan over high heat. When hot, add garlic, shallots, crawfish, tails, lima beans, asparagus, oregano, thyme, salt, and pepper. Sauté 2 to 3 minutes on high. Add butter to pan and let melt. Add flour and stir to coat evenly. Reduce heat to low and cook for another 10 minutes, stirring frequently. Increase heat back to high. Add shrimp and deglaze with stock. Bring to a boil. Reduce heat and simmer 3 to 4 minutes, until shrimp are done and stew is thickened and bubbly.

TO PLATE: *Place half of the ham in each bowl and divide stew into bowls.*

Andouille Sausage and Crawfish Gumbo with Cornbread

Yield: 1/2 gallon, 8 servings

Filé powder is ground sassafras leaves; it can be found in the spice section of most grocery stores.

4 tablespoons olive oil	1 teaspoon cayenne
1 pound diced andouille sausage	1 tablespoon dried thyme
2 cups diced onion	1 teaspoon dried oregano
1 cup diced green pepper	2 tablespoons minced garlic
1 cup diced red pepper	1 can (14.5 ounces) diced tomatoes
1 cup diced celery	5 cups fish stock (p. 2)
$\frac{1}{2}$ cup toasted flour (p. 3)	1 pound whole crawfish tails
1 tablespoon filé powder	2 batches JAX rice (p. 2)
$1\frac{1}{2}$ teaspoons kosher salt	8 whole crawfish
$1\frac{1}{2}$ teaspoons white pepper	Parsley sprigs for garnish
$1\frac{1}{2}$ teaspoons black pepper	

Place 2 tablespoons of the oil in large stockpot over medium-high heat. Add sausage and cook 5 to 6 minutes, until it starts to render. Add onion, green and red peppers, and celery. Cook vegetables for 8 to 10 minutes, stirring frequently. Add remaining 2 tablespoons of oil. Let heat through and then add flour. Reduce heat to medium-low and cook another 8 minutes, stirring frequently to prevent burning. Add filé powder, salt, white pepper, black pepper, cayenne, thyme, oregano, and garlic. Cook 5 to 6 minutes, stirring frequently until spices are toasted.

Deglaze with diced tomatoes. Cook 5 to 6 minutes, until juice has evaporated and tomatoes start to caramelize. Add fish stock and bring to a boil. Reduce heat and simmer for 30 minutes. Gumbo should get a thin gravy-like consistency. Add crawfish tails. Cook 5 minutes more.

TO PLATE: *Place a large scoop of JAX rice in center of each individual serving bowl. Ladle gumbo around rice. Stand a whole crawfish in rice and garnish with a parsley sprig. Serve with a square of cornbread.*

Cornbread

Yield: 12 pieces

- 2 cups flour
- 2 cups cornmeal
- $\frac{1}{4}$ cup sugar
- $\frac{1}{2}$ teaspoon kosher salt
- $1\frac{1}{2}$ tablespoons baking powder
- 1 teaspoon baking soda
- $1\frac{1}{2}$ cups buttermilk
- 1 cup low-fat milk
- 2 eggs
- 4 ounces (1 stick) melted butter

Preheat oven to 350ºF. Grease a 13 x 9 x 2-inch pan. Combine flour, cornmeal, sugar, salt, baking powder, and baking soda together in a large bowl. Whisk buttermilk, milk, and eggs in a small bowl. Whisk wet ingredients into dry. Stir in melted butter. Pour into greased pan. Bake 30 to 45 minutes or until center tests done. Let cool for 10 minutes. Cut into 12 pieces.

Crawfish Empanadas with Sun-Dried Cherry Ancho Dipping Sauce

Yield: 20 empanadas

Manchengo is a semi-soft Mexican cheese.

- 1 **cup masa corn flour**
- 2 **cups flour**
- $1\frac{1}{2}$ **teaspoons kosher salt, plus more for seasoning**
- 5 **eggs**
- 3 **tablespoons water**
- 3 **cooked and finely diced new potatoes**
- 1 **cup chopped crawfish tails**
- 1 **bunch minced cilantro**
- $\frac{1}{2}$ **finely diced onion**
- $\frac{1}{4}$ **cup honey**
- 1 **cup grated manchengo**
- $\frac{1}{2}$ **teaspoon cayenne**
- 1 **teaspoon Chimayo chili powder**
  Oil for frying
  Kosher salt and white pepper

FOR THE DOUGH: Place masa, flour, and 1 1/2 teaspoons salt in standing mixer fit with a paddle attachment. Mix briefly to combine. Add 4 eggs and 2 tablespoons water. Beat on medium speed for 5 minutes, until a stiff dough is formed. Let dough rest for 10 minutes. Beat remaining egg with remaining 1 tablespoon of water for egg wash.

FOR THE FILLING: Mix all remaining ingredients together in a large bowl. Preheat fryer to 375°F. Roll out dough as thin as possible to about 1/8-inch thickness. Using a 3-inch-diameter round cookie cutter, cut dough into 20 circles. Using a pastry brush, coat dough surface with egg wash. Place 1 tablespoon filling on each circle. Fold dough in half to make a half-moon shape and close edge with fork. Fry empanadas in small batches. Drain briefly on paper towels. Season with salt and pepper.

Sun-Dried Cherry Ancho Dipping Sauce

Yield: 2 cups

- 1 **cup sun-dried cherries**
- 2 **cups water**
- $\frac{1}{2}$ **cup brown sugar**
- $\frac{1}{2}$ **tablespoon ancho chili powder**
- $\frac{1}{4}$ **cup ketchup**
- $\frac{1}{2}$ **cup cider vinegar**
- $\frac{1}{4}$ **cup whiskey**
- $\frac{1}{2}$ **tablespoon black pepper**
- 1 **tablespoon cornstarch**

Place cherries and water in a small saucepot over medium-high heat. Bring to a boil. Reduce heat and simmer for 10 minutes. Cool. Puree in blender and strain through fine mesh sieve.

Place liquid back in pot with all remaining ingredients except for cornstarch. Bring to a boil and reduce by one quarter. Mix cornstarch with 2 tablespoons of cold water and stir into sauce. Increase heat and cook until thickened. Remove from heat.

 TO PLATE: *Place empanadas on a platter with a ramekin of warm Sun-Dried Cherry Ancho Dipping Sauce.*

37

Pan-Seared Grouper over Rock Shrimp Hash Browns with Sun-Dried Tomato Pesto

Yield: 4 servings

Rock shrimp come peeled; check to make sure they are deveined.

- 4 **tablespoons olive oil**
- 1 **small finely diced red onion**
- 1 **small finely diced green pepper**
- 1 **small finely diced red pepper**
- $\frac{1}{2}$ **pound rock shrimp**
- 2 **pounds cooked and diced new potatoes**
  Kosher salt and white pepper
- $\frac{1}{2}$ **bunch trimmed asparagus**
- $1\frac{1}{2}$ **pounds grouper, cut into 4 equal pieces**
- $\frac{1}{4}$ **cup white wine**
- $\frac{1}{2}$ **cup drained and rinsed capers**
- $\frac{1}{4}$ **cup chiffonade basil**
- 1 **zested and juiced lemon**
- 3 **tablespoons diced butter**

38

There are many different species of grouper. Some of the more popular types are jewfish, nassau, black, and red grouper; sometimes grouper is even marketed as bass. It is fished in the Gulf of Mexico, the Caribbean, and the South Pacific off the coasts of southern California, Mexico, and Central America. Many species of grouper undergo sex reversal, making sperm when young and later producing eggs. To spawn, they gather in large groups and in very specific places and times according to the phases of the moon. Most grouper is sold in Florida. It is low in fat, has flaky white meat, a very mild flavor, and a firm, meaty texture. Grouper is great for pan roasting or grilling.

Heat 2 tablespoons of the oil in large sauté pan over medium-high heat. Add onion, green pepper, and red pepper. Sauté vegetables 8 minutes until tender. Add rock shrimp and cook through, about 5 to 8 minutes. Add new potatoes; sear on all sides and season with salt and pepper. Keep warm. Bring a small pot of water to a boil, then blanch asparagus for about 3 minutes. Meanwhile, place 1 tablespoon of the oil in another large sauté pan and turn heat to high. Season grouper with salt and pepper. Place fish in pan and sear on one side, about 2 minutes. Flip over and deglaze pan with white wine. Add capers, basil, and lemon zest and juice.

gRoUpeR

Finish cooking fish, 3 minutes, and let pan sauce reduce slightly. Add butter and slowly swirl in. Drain asparagus; place in small bowl and toss with remaining tablespoon of olive oil and season with salt and pepper.

 TO PLATE: *Place a mound of hash browns in center bottom of plate. Place a few asparagus spears on each plate with bases on top of hash browns. Place grouper on top of asparagus bases. Pour pan sauce onto plates and drizzle Sun-Dried Tomato Pesto over fish.*

Sun-Dried Tomato Pesto

Yield: 1 cup

- $\frac{1}{2}$ cup sun-dried tomatoes
- 2 tablespoons roasted garlic, plus 1/2 cup oil (p. 3)
- $\frac{1}{4}$ cup toasted pine nuts
- $\frac{1}{4}$ cup grated Asiago cheese
- 2 tablespoons basil chiffonade
- $\frac{1}{4}$ teaspoon kosher salt
- $\frac{1}{2}$ teaspoon white pepper

Cover sun-dried tomatoes with hot water for 10 minutes to soften. Place softened tomatoes and liquid in blender or food processor and puree. Add roasted garlic, pine nuts, cheese, basil, salt, and pepper and puree. (It may be necessary to add a little more water.) With blender running slowly, drizzle in roasted garlic oil until pesto becomes too thick to incorporate any more. Pour into squeeze tube.

TO TOAST PINE NUTS: Place on baking sheet in 350°F oven until lightly browned.

39

GROUPER

Sesame-Tempura Crusted Halibut with Jasmine Rice Cakes and Green Curry

Yield: 6 servings

1 egg yolk

$\frac{1}{2}$ cup water

$\frac{2}{3}$ cup flour

$\frac{1}{4}$ cup cornstarch

$5\frac{1}{2}$ tablespoons sesame oil

2 tablespoons sesame seeds

$2\frac{1}{4}$ pounds halibut, cut into 6 equal pieces
   Kosher salt and white pepper

2 cups julienne snow peas

1 julienne red pepper

2 cups julienne shiitake mushrooms

2 cups chiffonade spinach
   Sweet soy sauce

TO MAKE TEMPURA BATTER: In a small bowl whisk together egg yolk and water. In another small bowl, whisk together flour and cornstarch. Add egg yolk and water, 1 1/2 tablespoons of the sesame oil, and sesame seeds to flour mixture. Whisk until smooth.

TO COOK HALIBUT: Preheat oven to 400°F. Season halibut with salt and white pepper. Place 3 tablespoons of sesame oil in a large, oven-safe sauté pan over medium-high heat. Dip halibut into tempura batter. Place gently in hot oil. Let cook 3 to 5 minutes on one side. Turn over, then place pan in oven and let bake for another 3 to 5 minutes. As the fish is cooking, heat remaining 1 tablespoon sesame oil in another sauté pan over medium-high heat. Add snow peas, red pepper, and mushrooms. Cook 3 to 5 minutes, until vegetables soften. Add spinach and turn quickly to wilt evenly. Remove fish from oven.

 TO PLATE: *Ladle 1/3 cup (roughly 3 ounces) Green Curry Coconut Cream onto each plate. Place one Jasmine Rice Cake in center of plate. Place sautéed vegetables in front of rice cake. Place halibut on top of rice cake. Drizzle with sweet soy sauce.*

In the flounder family, halibut is the largest flatfish. Three species, Atlantic, Pacific, and Greenland, are all left-eye dominant and can grow to six hundred pounds. Flatfish are born with one eye on each side of their bodies. After about sixty days, they turn and start to swim sideways, or parallel to the ocean floor. One eye migrates to the other side of the body, which looks upward, and that side of the fish turns darker; the other side, which faces the ocean floor, turns white to become less visible to predators. Halibut is fished off the Alaskan coasts in summer and is not available in winter. However, another species, called California halibut, is available in winter. It is right-eye dominant and fished off the coast of . . . guess where? California. And it is much smaller—up to only sixty pounds. The meat is similar—translucent white color and mild flavor but not as moist as Alaskan, nor as thick. Halibut is a delicate fish and is sometimes difficult to grill, so we recommend pan roasting or roasting in the oven.

hALibuT

Green Curry Coconut Cream

Yield: 2 1/2 cups

This sauce is pretty spicy. If you can't take the heat, you may want to reduce the amount of green curry paste.

- 2 cups heavy cream
- $\frac{1}{2}$ cup shredded or flaked coconut
- 1 tablespoon minced shallots
- 2 tablespoons minced garlic
- $\frac{1}{4}$ bunch chopped green onions
- $\frac{1}{4}$ diced onion
- $\frac{1}{4}$ bunch minced cilantro
- 1 cup fish stock (p. 2)
- $\frac{1}{4}$ cup chopped basil
- 1 teaspoon curry powder
- 2 tablespoons green curry paste
  Kosher salt and white pepper

Place all ingredients in a saucepan. Bring to a boil. Reduce heat and simmer 20 minutes. Let cool completely. Puree in small batches in blender and strain through chinois. When ready to serve, return sauce to saucepan and bring back to a boil; season with salt and pepper.

Jasmine Rice Cakes

Yield: 12 cakes, 6 servings

Jasmine is a delicately fragrant, white, long-grained variety of Thai rice. Make the rice a day ahead and the cakes just before serving.

- $\frac{1}{2}$ cup shredded or flaked coconut
- 2 cups milk
- 1$\frac{1}{2}$ cups jasmine rice
- 1 peeled, cooked, and mashed sweet potato
- 1 peeled, cooked, and mashed carrot
- $\frac{1}{2}$ teaspoon kosher salt
- $\frac{1}{2}$ teaspoon white pepper
- $\frac{1}{2}$ cup chopped basil
- $\frac{1}{2}$ bunch chopped cilantro
- 1 tablespoon honey
- 1 tablespoon sweet soy sauce
- 2 tablespoons olive oil

Place coconut and milk in a small saucepan. Bring to a boil. Reduce heat and simmer 30 minutes.

Add jasmine rice and bring back to a boil. Reduce heat to low and simmer another 15 minutes until rice is cooked. Stir the rice frequently so it does not burn. When rice is cooked, stir in sweet potato, carrot, salt, pepper, basil, cilantro, honey, and sweet soy sauce; combine thoroughly. Spread rice onto a baking sheet and let cool.

Form patties out of the rice mixture with an ice cream scoop or your hands. They should be about 2 1/2 inches in diameter and 1/2-inch thick. Heat oil on a griddle or in a sauté pan. Place cakes on hot griddle and cook 4 to 6 minutes per side, until golden brown.

Rhumba's Garam-Masala Crusted Halibut with Candied Ginger Beurre Blan

Yield: 8 servings

You will have garam masala left over—keep it in a spice jar, tightly sealed. If you aren't feeling ambitious enough to make your own, you can buy garam masala already blended in the spice section of your local grocery store.

12 decorticated cardamom pods, husks removed

$\frac{1}{4}$ cup black peppercorns

3 tablespoons cumin seed

2 tablespoons coriander seed

3 cloves

$\frac{1}{2}$ teaspoon cinnamon

$\frac{1}{2}$ cup red wine vinegar

$\frac{1}{4}$ cup sugar

2 tablespoons minced gingerroot

$\frac{1}{2}$ cup white wine

2 cups heavy cream

$\frac{1}{2}$ pound (2 sticks) diced butter

Kosher salt and white pepper

2 pounds halibut, cut into 8 equal pieces

2 tablespoons olive oil

2 bunches cleaned and coarsely chopped spinach

3 tablespoons Bird Pepper Vinaigrette

$\frac{1}{2}$ cup wasabi powder

2 tablespoons lime juice

TO MAKE THE GARAM MASALA: Preheat oven to 350°F. Place cardamom pods, peppercorns, cumin, coriander, and cloves on a sheet tray. Place in oven and toast for 5 to 10 minutes, until very fragrant. Remove from oven—let cool. Add cinnamon and grind.

TO MAKE THE CANDIED GINGER BEURRE BLANC: Place vinegar, sugar, and ginger in a small saucepan. Bring to a boil. Reduce heat and let simmer until pan is almost dry. It may be necessary to turn down the heat—this sauce can

burn easily and must be watched carefully. Add white wine; again reduce until pan is almost dry. Add cream and reduce by half. Turn the heat to low and slowly whisk in the butter, one piece at a time. The sauce should get a slightly thickened glossy consistency. When all the butter is incorporated, season with salt and pepper. Pour candied ginger beurre blanc through fine mesh strainer and into a squeeze tube.

TO COOK THE HALIBUT: Season halibut with salt and white pepper and then place top side down in garam masala. Place 1 tablespoon of the oil in a large sauté pan over high heat. When hot, add fish, crust side down. Cook 4 minutes to sear topside. Turn over and cook another 3 to 5 minutes. Heat remaining 1 tablespoon of oil over high heat in a medium-size sauté pan. Add spinach and wilt with 3 tablespoons of Bird Pepper Vinegar; adjust the spice to your liking. Season with salt and pepper. In a small bowl, mix wasabi powder with a little lime juice at a time, it should become the consistency of play dough. Let rest 10 minutes. If it is too dry, add a little more lime juice; if it is too wet, add a little more wasabi powder. Form into 8 small balls.

 TO PLATE: *Place 1 wasabi ball on each plate. Place a large scoop of Yucca Whipped Potatoes in center of each plate. Place fish on top of potatoes and Apricot Blatjang on top of fish. Place spinach to the left and right of fish. Drizzle Candied Ginger Beurre Blanc over fish and at top and bottom of plate.*

42

Apricot Blatjang

Yield: 2 1/2 cups

Blatjang is a West African dried fruit chutney.

2   cups halved dried apricots
½   small finely diced onion
½   cup cider vinegar
1   teaspoon toasted and ground coriander seed
1   tablespoon minced ginger
1   seeded and finely diced jalapeño
1   zested and juiced lemon
    Kosher salt and white pepper

Place all ingredients in a small saucepot and cover with water. Bring to a boil. Reduce heat and simmer until apricots are plump and have soaked up most of the liquid, about 15 minutes. Season with salt and pepper.

Bird Pepper Vinegar

Yield: 1/2 cup

If you can't find bird peppers, you can substitute pequins.

½   cup sherry vinegar
1   halved Scotch bonnet chili
6   bird peppers

Put vinegar, chili halves, and peppers in a small saucepan. Bring to a boil. Remove from heat and let steep for at least 1 hour. Strain out chili and bird peppers.

Yucca Whipped Potatoes

2   peeled and chopped yuccas (the size of large Idahoes)
6   peeled and chopped large Idaho potatoes
1   cup heavy cream
1   cup buttermilk
2   ounces (1/2 stick) butter
2   tablespoons roasted garlic (p. 3)
1   teaspoon kosher salt
1   teaspoon white pepper

Bring two large pots of water to a boil. Cook yuccas 18 to 20 minutes in one and potatoes 12 to 15 minutes in another until fork-tender. Drain. Bring heavy cream, buttermilk, butter, and garlic to a boil. Reduce by one-third. In a large bowl, mash cooked yucca and potatoes together. Add hot cream mixture to desired consistency and season with salt and pepper.

43

Pan-Seared John Dory with Portobello Ricotta Ravioli and Lobster Broth

Yield: 6 servings

John Dory is a very small fish. Try to get six- to eight-ounce fillets.

- **2 tablespoons flour**
- **1 teaspoon kosher salt**
- **1 teaspoon white pepper**
- **2 tablespoons chopped parsley**
- **2$\frac{1}{4}$ pounds John Dory fillets**
- **1 tablespoon olive oil**

In a small bowl, mix together flour, salt, pepper, and parsley. Dredge fish in flour mixture.

Place oil in a large sauté pan over high heat. When almost smoking hot, add fish topside down (nonskin side). Let sear 2 to 3 minutes, until nicely browned. Turn fish and finish cooking 1 to 2 more minutes.

 TO PLATE: *Place 4 Portobello Ricotta Ravioli in shallow serving bowls with 1/2 cup of snow peas. Pour 1/2 cup (4 ounces) of Lobster Broth over ravioli. Place fish on top of ravioli and top with lobster relish.*

Lobster Broth

Yield: 4 cups

- **1 tablespoon olive oil**
- **1 chopped onion**
- **2 cups chopped celery**
- **2 peeled and chopped carrots**
- **1 clove peeled and crushed garlic**
- **$\frac{1}{2}$ bunch chopped parsley**
- **3 sprigs thyme**
- **3 sprigs oregano**
- **2 bay leaves**
- **1 tablespoon cracked black peppercorns**
- **1 gallon water**
- **1$\frac{1}{2}$ pounds live Maine lobster**
- **Ice water bath**
- **1 tablespoon olive oil**
- **1 zested lemon**
- **$\frac{1}{4}$ teaspoon kosher salt**

Place oil in large stockpot over high heat. Add onion, celery, and carrots. Sauté 2 to 3 minutes. Reduce heat and cook 20 minutes. Add garlic, parsley, thyme, oregano, bay leaves, and cracked peppercorns. Cook for 2 to 3 minutes. Add water and bring to a boil. Add lobster. Let water return to a boil and then reduce heat to poach lobster for 10 minutes. Remove lobster from pot and immerse in ice water bath to stop cooking process, about 10 minutes, until cold. See tip on page 46 to remove meat from shell. Return lobster poaching water to a boil and let reduce by three quarters. Strain through a fine chinois and reserve the broth.

TO MAKE LOBSTER RELISH: Mix lobster meat with olive oil, lemon zest, and salt.

Portobello Ricotta Ravioli

Yield: 40 ravioli

There will be extra ravioli—they freeze well. Just make sure you lay them out flat, not touching each other, until they are frozen so they don't stick together. .

- ½ gallon low-fat milk
- 4 cups buttermilk
- 1 cup heavy cream
- ½ cup chiffonade basil
- ½ tablespoon kosher salt, plus 1 teaspoon
- ½ tablespoon black pepper, plus 1 teaspoon
- 1 tablespoon olive oil
- ½ finely diced red onion
- 1 tablespoon minced garlic
- 1 tablespoon minced shallots
- 1 tablespoon minced thyme
- 1 tablespoon minced oregano
- 1 tablespoon minced parsley
- 3 diced portobello mushrooms
- ½ cup Lobster Broth
- ½ cup grated Asiago cheese
- 1 egg
- 1 tablespoon water
- 20 egg roll skins
- Flour for dusting
- 3 cups julienne snow peas

TO MAKE RICOTTA: Whisk milk, buttermilk, cream, basil, 1/2 tablespoon salt, and 1/2 tablespoon black pepper together in a small pot. Bring to a boil to scald cream mixture. Remove from heat and let rest 20 minutes. To remove curd from milk mixture, pour through a large fine mesh strainer or place several layers of cheesecloth in a large colander. Let drain for 1 hour.

TO MAKE RAVIOLI STUFFING: Place oil in a large sauté pan over medium-high heat. When pan is very hot, add onion, garlic, shallots, thyme, oregano, parsley, and remaining salt and pepper. Sauté 2 to 3 minutes. Add mushrooms and cook until liquid evaporates from pan. Deglaze with 1/2 cup Lobster Broth and again let cook until pan is almost dry. Be sure to scrape pan and remove mushroom bits from bottom. Let this mixture cool completely. Mix together cooled, drained ricotta, mushroom mixture, and cheese.

TO MAKE RAVIOLI: Beat egg in a small bowl with water. Place an egg roll skin on flour-dusted work surface. Dip pastry brush in egg wash, and brush egg roll skin. Mentally draw a "+"on the skin. Place 1 tablespoon of filling in the center of each of the four quadrants. Place another egg roll skin on top. Press down with index finger from the center out to remove air and seal skins together. Make sure there are no air bubbles. Using a fluted pastry wheel, cut the + you mentally drew through the skin and around the outside of skin to seal the edges. Place finished ravioli on a flour-dusted cookie sheet. You can stack layers of ravioli on floured sheets of waxed paper. Refrigerate or freeze until ready to prepare. Boil ravioli in Lobster Broth for 3 to 5 minutes. Again, make sure edges are sealed or the ravioli will burst when cooking. You will probably have to cook them in batches; remove with a slotted spoon. When finished cooking ravioli, place snow peas in strainer and blanch in boiling Lobster Broth until bright green, about 2 to 3 minutes.

45

John Dory is found from the Atlantic to the coasts of New Zealand. In France it is called St. Pierre; legend has it that the spot found on its side is the thumbprint of St. Peter. John Dory has been called a baby halibut, and its delicate white fillets definitely are comparable. Pan searing is best for this fish, and it should be slightly floured before cooking to avoid sticking.

JoHn DoRY

HOW TO BOIL A LOBSTER: Use at least one gallon of water for a 1 1/4-pound lobster. Bring to a rolling boil. Add lobster, then when water returns to a boil, turn down heat to medium-high and let the lobster poach 6 minutes for the first pound and two minutes for each additional pound.

TO REMOVE LOBSTER MEAT FROM SHELL: Twist tail to remove it from body. Lay tail flat on cutting board. Place French knife on top of tail and cut all the way through so there are 2 pieces. Pull meat from shell. Grasp claw and twist to remove it along with knuckles (arm). Place an old kitchen towel over the claw. Turn the blade over and give the claw a firm whack to crack shell. Remove meat. Do the same with each of the knuckles. Coarsely chop meat.

A lobster takes five to seven years to mature to a one-pound size. There are basically two kinds, American lobster (with claws) and spiny lobster (without claws). The American lobster is found off the coast of the North Atlantic, and the spiny lobster off the South Atlantic. In the Rocky Mountain region, you will most likely find American lobster, but just make sure it is live and fresh. When you pick it up it should thrash around a little—the livelier the fresher!

LoBsTeR

Lobster Bisque

Yield: 1/2 gallon

This will take some time to make. You will want to make it a day ahead so it can cool before pureeing and straining. Save leftover soup; it makes a great sauce for fish or chicken.

- 1 gallon water, plus additional cold water for ice bath
- Ice
- $1\frac{1}{2}$ pounds live Maine lobster
- 2 tablespoons olive oil
- 2 cups coarsely chopped leeks
- 1 cup coarsely chopped onion
- 1 cup coarsely chopped celery
- 1 cup coarsely chopped carrots
- 2 bay leaves
- 2 tablespoons minced garlic
- 2 tablespoons minced shallots
- 2 tablespoons dried basil
- 2 tablespoons dried thyme
- 1 tablespoon black peppercorns
- 2 tablespoons tomato paste
- 1 tablespoon JAX Old Bay Seafood Seasoning
- 1 teaspoon celery seed
- 2 teaspoons kosher salt
- $\frac{1}{2}$ cup long-grain white rice
- 4 tablespoons brandy
- 2 cups heavy cream
- 2 (14.5-ounce) cans diced tomatoes
- Freshly ground black pepper

Bring 1 gallon of water to a boil in a large stockpot. While water is heating, fill a bowl (large enough to fit lobster) full of ice and then fill with cold water. This is your ice bath. When water is boiling, place lobster in pot and cook approximately 3 minutes, until it stops moving. Remove lobster from water with tongs and plunge into ice bath for 5 minutes. Remove lobster meat from the shell. With a French knife, cut the lobster body in half lengthwise. Set aside lobster body, shells, and any juices from the cutting board. Return lobster cooking water to a boil and let reduce by three fourths. This will be the stock for the bisque. Dice lobster meat. This will be the garnish for the soup.

Place oil in a large stockpot over medium-high heat. Add lobster body, shells, and juices. Sear for approximately 5 to 6 minutes, stirring frequently. Add leeks, onion, celery, carrots, bay leaves, garlic, shallots, basil, and thyme. Reduce heat to medium and sauté approximately 15 to 20 minutes. The vegetables will release liquid; just keep stirring until all liquid has evaporated and pan is almost dry. Reduce heat to medium-low. Add peppercorns, tomato paste, JAX Old Bay Seafood Seasoning, celery seed, salt, and rice. Sauté for approximately 10 minutes, until tomato paste caramelizes and turns darker, slightly brown. Again, stir frequently, as the mixture will be dry.

Deglaze with 2 tablespoons brandy and add lobster stock (4 cups), cream, and tomatoes. Bring to a boil. Reduce heat to medium and let simmer for 30 minutes. Remove from heat. Let cool completely. You may want to let this cool overnight.

Remove lobster body from bisque. Take care not to miss any lobster body parts—they may ruin your blender. Place in small batches in blender. Fill blender about three-fourths full. Spin on high setting until smooth then strain through chinois or fine mesh strainer. A large ladle is a good tool to help force the bisque through the chinois. When all bisque has been spun and strained, place back in large stockpot on stove. Bring to a boil. Add remaining brandy and reserved lobster meat. Bring back to a boil. Reduce heat and let simmer 3 minutes. Check seasonings.

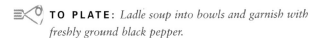 **TO PLATE**: *Ladle soup into bowls and garnish with freshly ground black pepper.*

Lobster Pot Pie

Yield: 6 servings

For directions on how to remove lobster meat from shell, see tip on page 46.

- 1 **gallon water**
- 2 **1 1/2-pound lobsters**
  Ice water bath
- 1 **tablespoon olive oil**
- 1 **small diced onion**
- 1 **small sliced leek**
- 3 **stalks diced celery**
- 3 **peeled and diced carrots**
- 5 **tablespoons butter**
- 5 **tablespoons flour**
- 2 **cups peeled and diced Idaho potatoes**
- 2 **tablespoons minced thyme**
- 1 **teaspoon kosher salt**
- $\frac{1}{2}$ **teaspoon black pepper**
- 2 **cups chopped asparagus**
- 1 **package (1.1 pounds) puff pastry, 2 rectangular sheets**
- 1 **beaten egg**
- 1 **tablespoon water**

Preheat oven to 425°F. Place water in a large stockpot and bring to a boil. Add lobsters and let water return to a boil. Reduce heat to poach lobsters for 10 minutes. Remove lobsters from pot and cool in ice water bath. Remove meat and coarsely chop (2 cups). Bring water back to a boil and let liquid reduce by half. Set lobster water aside.

Place oil in a large saucepan over high heat. Add onion, leek, and celery. Sauté vegetables until soft and slightly caramelized, 10 to 12 minutes. Add carrots and butter. After butter has melted, add flour. Reduce heat to medium-low and cook 12 to 15 minutes, stirring frequently until flour is absorbed and slightly toasted; it should start to

smell nutty. Return heat to high, deglaze with lobster water, then add potatoes, thyme, salt, and pepper. Bring to a boil. Reduce heat and let simmer 40 minutes, until carrots and potatoes are cooked and broth is thickened and gravy-like in consistency. Add asparagus.

TO PLATE: *You can put the pot pies in one large or several individual ungreased dishes that are oven-safe. Place the dish(es) upside down on top of one sheet of puff pastry. With a pastry wheel or knife, cut around the edge of the dish, so that the puff pastry is slightly bigger, 1/2 inch, than the dish itself. Pour hot pot pie mix into dish(es). Place puff pastry on top. Whisk together egg and water. Brush top of puff pastry with egg wash. Let bake 10 to 15 minutes, until pastry puffs and is golden brown. Take care to let puff pastry cook completely before removing from oven or it will deflate. Serve immediately.*

48

Lobster Mulligatawny

Yield: 1/2 gallon, 8 servings

Mulligatawny is derived from the East Indian word *milag-utannir* for "pepper water." This spicy soup has many variations with lamb, chicken, or rabbit (ours, of course, has lobster), and it usually has curry powder and sometimes even apples. Most good seafood counters have prepackaged lobster meat to buy; if you can't find any, buy a live lobster and see the tips on page 46 for how to cook it and remove the meat.

- 1 **tablespoon olive oil**
- 2 **small finely diced onions**
- 1 **bunch finely diced celery**
- 2 **small finely diced green peppers**
- 2 **cups peeled and finely diced carrots**
- 1 **can (14.5 ounces) diced tomatoes**
- $\frac{1}{2}$ **pound (1/2 stick) butter**
- $\frac{1}{2}$ **cup flour**
- 1 **crushed clove**
- $\frac{1}{2}$ **teaspoon cayenne**
- 2 **teaspoons curry powder**
- $\frac{1}{4}$ **teaspoon nutmeg**
- $\frac{1}{4}$ **teaspoon turmeric**
- $\frac{1}{2}$ **teaspoon white pepper, plus extra for seasoning whipped cream**
- $1\frac{1}{2}$ **tablespoons kosher salt, plus extra for seasoning whipped cream**
- 1 **cup white wine**
- $\frac{1}{2}$ **cup apple cider**
- $1\frac{1}{2}$ **cups heavy cream**
- 4 **cups fish stock (p. 2)**
- $\frac{1}{2}$ **pound lobster meat**
- 1 **tablespoon minced cilantro**
- 1 **tablespoon lemon juice**

Place oil in stockpot over medium-high heat. Add onion, celery, and green peppers. Sauté vegetables until tender, about 10 minutes. Add carrots and tomatoes. Cook until liquid evaporates from tomatoes and pan is almost dry. Add butter and let melt. Reduce heat and add flour. Cook 10 to 12 minutes until vegetables are coated and flour has toasted; stir frequently to avoid burning the flour. Add clove, cayenne, curry powder, nutmeg, turmeric, white pepper, and salt. Let spices toast 3 to 5 minutes, stirring frequently to prevent them from burning. Increase heat back to high, deglaze with wine, then add cider, 1 cup cream, and fish stock. Bring to a boil. Reduce heat and let simmer 20 to 30 minutes, until thickened. Add lobster meat. Heat through. In a small bowl, whip remaining cream with cilantro, lemon juice, and dashes of salt and white pepper.

49

 TO PLATE: *In the center of each bowl of soup, add a dollop of the whipped cream.*

Lobster Club with Baked Lemon Aioli and JAX Chips

Yield: 2 servings

You can buy cooked lobster meat at most seafood counters. If you can't find it, just buy a live lobster and follow the tips on page 46 for instructions on cooking and removing the meat.

- **6 slices (1-inch thick) of brioche**
- **½ cup Baked Lemon Aioli**
- **2 cups arugula**
- **6 strips crispy applewood-smoked bacon, cut in half**
- **½ pound cooked lobster meat**

Toast brioche and slather each slice with Baked Lemon Aioli. For each sandwich, lay arugula on top of brioche, then 3 half-strips of bacon, and one-fourth of the lobster meat. Place another slice of the brioche on top of the lobster then arugula, 3 strips of bacon, and one-fourth of the lobster meat. Top with a third slice of brioche. Each sandwich should have 3 slices of brioche with one-fourth of the arugula, bacon, and lobster meat between them.

 TO PLATE: *Cut sandwich in quarters and place on plates with JAX Chips.*

Baked Lemon Aioli

Yield: 1 1/4 cups

Pasteurized egg yolks can be found in the dairy case in most grocery stores.

- **3 lemons**
- **1 pasteurized egg yolk**
- **1 tablespoon mashed roasted garlic (p. 3)**
- **¼ teaspoon kosher salt**
- **⅛ teaspoon white pepper**
- **1 cup olive oil**
- **¼ cup chopped kalamata olives**
- **1½ tablespoons capers**

Preheat oven to 350°F. Place lemons in an oven-safe dish and bake 30 to 45 minutes until slightly golden and soft. Remove from oven and cool. Squeeze 2 1/2 tablespoons of lemon juice into bowl of food processor. Add egg yolk, garlic, salt, and pepper and blend until pale yellow in color. With food processor running, slowly add oil in a thin stream. Place in a small bowl and stir in olives and capers. Aioli should be the consistency of thin mayonnaise.

JAX Chips

Yield: 4 servings

Serve these with any of our fabulous sandwiches.

Oil for frying	**1 teaspoon kosher salt**
Pinch cayenne	**¼ teaspoon white pepper**
¼ teaspoon paprika	**1 large Idaho potato**
⅛ teaspoon cinnamon	**1 large sweet potato**

Preheat fryer to 350°F. Mix together cayenne, paprika, cinnamon, salt, and pepper.

Peel potatoes. Using your vegetable peeler, cut long, thin, wide strips of each type of potato. It's important to keep them a uniform thickness. Keep separate, and fry in small batches separately; sweet potatoes take a little longer to cook. Drain on paper towels and season with spice mixture. Mix chips together and serve.

Tamarind-Glazed Mahi Mahi with Sweet Potato Black Bean Cakes and Banan

Yield: 3 cups of glaze, 6 servings of fish

Tamarind paste can be found in Asian markets. There will be leftover glaze; it will keep refrigerated, tightly sealed, for weeks.

Oil for frying	3 tablespoons honey
8 ounces tamarind paste	3 ounces spiced rum
4 cups water	$\frac{1}{2}$ teaspoon Chimayo chili powder
$\frac{1}{2}$ stick cinnamon	$\frac{1}{2}$ teaspoon cumin
2 bay leaves	$\frac{1}{4}$ cup brown sugar
$\frac{1}{2}$ teaspoon allspice	$2\frac{1}{4}$ pounds mahi mahi, cut into 6 equal pieces
$\frac{1}{2}$ teaspoon ground ginger	Kosher salt and white pepper
3 tablespoons molasses	1 julienne sweet potato (matchstick-size pieces)

Clean and oil surface of gas or charcoal grill, then preheat. Preheat deep fryer to 325°F. Place all ingredients except mahi mahi, salt, pepper, and sweet potato in a small saucepan and bring to a boil. Reduce heat and simmer 20 minutes, until tamarind paste starts to separate. Mash paste with a fork. Remove from heat and let cool. Remove bay leaves and cinnamon stick and puree paste in blender, then strain through fine mesh sieve.

Season mahi mahi with salt and pepper. Place fish on hot grill surface. Let cook 3 to 5 minutes. Turn over and brush with tamarind glaze. Let finish cooking 2 to 3 minutes more. Meanwhile, cook the sweet potato garnish, placing a small amount—a cup or so at a time—in fry basket. Cook 5 to 8 minutes, until potatoes are crispy. Drain on layered paper towels. Season with salt.

52

Mahi mahi is the Hawaiian name for the fish in the mackerel family referred to as dolphinfish (not related to the mammal) or dorado. It is a warm-water fish and is caught off the coasts of Florida and southern California down through to South America and Hawaii. Mahi mahi is a fast-growing fish, maturing in four years, and it grows from ten to fifty pounds and six feet long. When it is very fresh, it has a yellow streak along the belly, sometimes even blue streaks. The flesh is dark white with brown streaks and turns white when cooked. It has a medium texture and mild flavor. This is a very versatile fish, which is great on the grill.

 TO PLATE: *Ladle 1/4 cup (2 ounces) of Banana Green Curry onto each plate (or into shallow bowls). Place 2 Sweet Potato Black Bean Cakes in center of each plate. Place fish on top of cakes and garnish with fried sweet potato.*

MaHi MaHi

Sweet Potato Black Bean Cakes
Yield: 16 cakes

1 cup uncooked black beans, soaked in cold water overnight
1 tablespoon minced garlic
1 tablespoon minced shallots
1 teaspoon black pepper
3 peeled and diced sweet potatoes
1 peeled and diced Idaho potato
2 bay leaves
3 cloves
2 tablespoons roasted and pureed garlic (p. 3)
2 tablespoons brown sugar
1 teaspoon cumin
1 teaspoon ground ginger
$\frac{1}{2}$ teaspoon chili flakes
$\frac{1}{8}$ teaspoon nutmeg
$\frac{1}{4}$ teaspoon cinnamon
$\frac{1}{2}$ teaspoon kosher salt
1 tablespoon olive oil

Drain black beans and place in a small saucepot with garlic, shallots, and pepper. Cover with water by 2 inches and bring to a boil. Reduce heat to simmer and cook until beans are tender, about 2 hours; you may have to add more water. Drain and rinse. Bring a large pot of water to a boil. Cook potatoes with bay leaves and cloves until tender. Drain in colander, remove bay leaves and cloves, and mash potatoes in a large bowl. Add roasted garlic, brown sugar, cumin, ginger, chili flakes, nutmeg, cinnamon, and salt to bowl and mix thoroughly. Fold in black beans. Place oil in a large sauté pan or griddle over medium-high heat. Drop large rounded tablespoons of potato bean mixture onto griddle and cook until golden brown. Flip cakes over, flatten with a spatula, and cook 2 to 3 more minutes. Keep cakes warm in a 200°F oven.

Banana Green Curry
Yield: 2 1/2 cups

$\frac{1}{2}$ tablespoon green curry paste
1 tablespoon minced garlic
1 tablespoon minced shallots
$\frac{1}{2}$ zested and juiced lemon
$\frac{1}{2}$ zested and juiced lime
Pinch cinnamon
1 cup fish stock (p. 2)
1 cup heavy cream
1 bay leaf
$\frac{1}{2}$ tablespoon brown sugar
$\frac{1}{4}$ teaspoon turmeric
$\frac{1}{2}$ very ripe banana
$\frac{1}{2}$ tablespoon basil chiffonade
Kosher salt and white pepper

Place all ingredients except banana and basil in a large pot and bring to a boil. Reduce heat and simmer for 10 minutes. Add banana and basil. Let cool. Place in blender and puree. Pour through fine mesh strainer and reheat. Season with salt and pepper.

53

Rosemary-Skewered Mahi Mahi with Potato "Risotto" and Caramelized Onio

Yield: 4 servings

- 1½ pounds mahi mahi, cut into 2-inch cubes
- 1 pint grape tomatoes
- 2 zucchini, cut into 1-inch rounds
- 2 tablespoons olive oil
- ½ teaspoon kosher salt
- ¼ teaspoon freshly ground black pepper
- 4 fresh rosemary sprigs

Soak eight wooden skewers in water for 20 minutes. Clean and oil charcoal or gas grill surface, then preheat. Place mahi mahi, tomatoes, and zucchini rounds in a large bowl. Toss with oil, salt, and pepper. Spear fish and vegetables onto skewers, alternating mahi mahi, tomato, and zucchini. Add rosemary to skewers by sticking sprigs next to skewer and into cubes of fish. Place skewers onto hot grill surface. Cook about 3 minutes per side.

 TO PLATE: *Place Potato "Risotto" in center of each plate. Ladle Caramelized Onion Reduction around potatoes to cover base of plate, and crisscross skewers on top of potatoes.*

Caramelized Onion Reduction

Yield: 4 cups

You will want to make this a day ahead—it is simple but takes a long time.

- 4 pounds veal bones
- 1 coarsely chopped onion
- 3 coarsely chopped celery stalks
- 3 peeled and coarsely chopped carrots
- 2 tablespoons tomato paste
- 3 tablespoons olive oil
- 1 cup red wine
- 1 tablespoon dried thyme
- 1 tablespoon dried oregano
- 1 tablespoon black peppercorns
- 2 bay leaves
- 1 gallon water
- 4 large thinly sliced onions
- Kosher salt
- Freshly ground black pepper

Preheat oven to 350°F. Place veal bones in a roasting pan and set in the oven. Roast for 60 minutes. Add onion, celery, and carrots and roast another 30 minutes. Add tomato paste and roast 15 minutes more. Remove from oven. Place 2 tablespoons olive oil in a large stockpot over high heat. Add bones and vegetables and let them sizzle for 5 minutes, stirring occasionally. Deglaze with wine. Add thyme, oregano, peppercorns, and bay leaves. Fill pot with the water and bring to a boil. Reduce heat to barely a simmer. Simmer uncovered for 8 hours. Skim foam from the top as necessary.

Meanwhile, place remaining 1 tablespoon of oil in large sauté pan over medium-high heat. When hot, add onions. Sauté over high heat for 5 to 6 minutes until onions have "sweated out" their liquid and begun to caramelize. Reduce heat to medium and continue cooking. Onions should begin to darken in color. Keep cooking and reducing heat as necessary to get onions to a very dark brown color. After about 45 minutes, there should be about 2 cups of caramelized onions. Let onions cool completely.

Let stock rest and cool overnight in pot. Strain out bones and vegetables and place liquid in another stockpot, reserving 1/2 cup. Reduce liquid in stockpot by half. Place caramelized onions in a blender with 1/2 cup of reserved stock. Puree until smooth and strain into sauce when it has finished reducing. Season with salt and pepper.

54

Potato "Risotto"

This is not a traditional risotto made with arborio rice. Idaho potatoes are cooked slowly to release their starches, so the potatoes have a risotto-like consistency.

Yield: 4 servings

$\frac{1}{4}$ cup minced bacon

4 large peeled and finely diced Idaho potatoes

1 teaspoon kosher salt

Freshly ground black pepper

$\frac{1}{4}$ cup white wine

2 cups fish stock (p. 2)

$\frac{1}{2}$ cup heavy cream

$\frac{1}{2}$ cup grated Asiago cheese

Place bacon in large sauté pan over medium-high heat and render until crispy. Add potatoes and season with salt and pepper. Cook 5 minutes, then deglaze with wine. Reduce heat to medium. Cover and cook, stirring frequently until most of the liquid has evaporated. Add 1/2 cup of stock, cooking and stirring frequently until liquid has evaporated. Continue adding stock 1/2 cup at a time, cooking and stirring frequently until potatoes are soft. Keep a lid covering about three-fourths of the pan—this will steam the potatoes and speed up the cooking process. Add cream and cook, stirring frequently for about 5 minutes, until cream has reduced by three fourths. Add cheese and cook a few minutes more until cheese has melted. Check seasonings.

MAHI MAHI

55

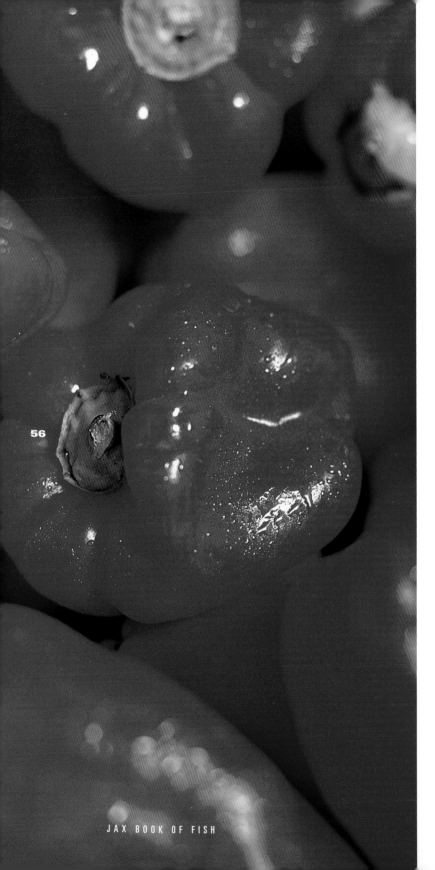

56

Grilled Mahi Mahi over Orzo Sala

Yield: 6 servings

1 tablespoon roasted garlic (p. 3)

1 tablespoon Dijon mustard

1 zested and juiced lemon

4 roasted shallots (p. 3)

1 cup roasted shallot oil, plus

   2 tablespoons (p. 3)

1 peeled eggplant

   Kosher salt

$2\frac{1}{4}$ pounds mahi mahi, cut into 6 equal portions

   Olive oil

   White pepper

$\frac{1}{2}$ pound cooked, drained, and rinsed orzo pasta

2 roasted, peeled, and julienned red peppers (p. 13)

1 bunch blanched and chopped asparagus

$\frac{1}{4}$ cup capers

$\frac{1}{4}$ cup pitted and chopped kalamata olives

8 ounces crumbled feta cheese

2 tablespoons minced thyme

$\frac{1}{2}$ cup beurre blanc, optional (p. 1)

Clean and oil surface of charcoal or gas grill, then preheat.

TO MAKE ROASTED SHALLOT VINAIGRETTE: Place garlic, mustard, lemon zest and juice, and shallots in blender. Puree. While the blender is running, slowly drizzle in 1 cup shallot oil.

TO GRILL EGGPLANT AND FISH: Cut eggplant into 1/2-inch-thick slices and place on sheet pan. Season with salt;

this will release the bitter juices of the eggplant and takes about 30 minutes. Soak up moisture with paper towels. Brush eggplant slices with 2 tablespoons roasted shallot oil. Place on hot grill and cook 3 to 5 minutes per side. Remove from heat. Let cool and dice. Brush the fish with olive oil and season with salt and white pepper. Grill 3 to 5 minutes per side depending on thickness of fish.

TO MAKE ORZO SALAD: Combine eggplant, orzo, red peppers, asparagus, capers, olives, feta, and thyme in a large bowl. Dress orzo salad with roasted shallot vinaigrette to taste. Season with salt and white pepper.

 TO PLATE: *Place scoop of Orzo Salad in center of each plate. Place fish on top of salad. Drizzle with beurre blanc, Roasted Red Pepper Vinaigrette, and Balsamic Reduction.*

Roasted Red Pepper Vinaigrette
Yield: 1 1/2 cups

> 2   roasted red peppers (p. 13)
> 1   tablespoon roasted garlic,
>   plus 1/2 cup oil (p. 3)
> 1   tablespoon minced shallots
> 1   tablespoon Dijon mustard
> 2   tablespoons red wine vinegar
> $\frac{1}{2}$ teaspoon kosher salt
> $\frac{1}{4}$ teaspoon white pepper

Place peppers, garlic, shallots, mustard, vinegar, salt, and pepper in a blender. Puree until smooth. Slowly drizzle in oil until thickened. Pour into a squeeze tube.

Balsamic Reduction
Yield: 1/4 cup

This is a very strong reduction—use only a little on each plate.

> 1   cup balsamic vinegar
> 1   tablespoon molasses

Place balsamic vinegar and molasses in small saucepot. Bring to a boil and reduce to 1/4 cup. Pour into squeeze tube.

57

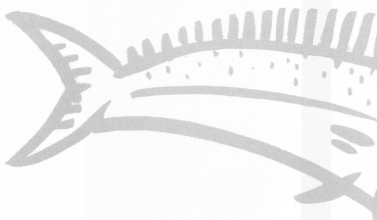

MAHI MAHI

Prosciutto-Wrapped Monkfish

Yield: 6 servings

2¼ pounds monkfish (six 6-ounce tails)
   Kosher salt and white pepper
6 thin slices of prosciutto
1 tablespoon olive oil

Preheat oven to 400°F. Season fish with salt and pepper. Lay prosciutto out on a flat surface. Place one portion of monkfish on each slice of prosciutto. Roll prosciutto slice tightly around fish and secure with a toothpick. Place oil in large sauté pan over high heat. Set monkfish in pan and let sear on one side, 2 to 3 minutes. Turn and place in oven to roast 3 to 4 minutes.

 TO PLATE: *Ladle 1/3 cup (roughly 3 ounces) of Portobello Reduction onto each plate. Place large square of Zucchini, Caramelized Leek, and Potato Gratin in center of plate. Place fish on top of gratin.*

58

Zucchini, Caramelized Leek, and Potato Gratin

Yield: 8 pieces

1 tablespoon olive oil
3 large thinly sliced leeks
6 peeled and thinly sliced Idaho potatoes
2 grated zucchini
1 cup heavy cream
2 cups grated Gruyère cheese
   Kosher salt
   Freshly ground black pepper

Preheat oven to 350°F. Heat oil in sauté pan. Add leeks and sauté 2 to 3 minutes. Decrease heat to medium and continue cooking until leeks start caramelizing. Cook 25 minutes more until dark brown in color and completely caramelized. Remove from heat. Layer potatoes on a 9 x 13-inch jelly roll pan with 1/2-inch-deep sides. Place grated zucchini on top of potatoes. Drizzle cream over all of potatoes. Top zucchini with caramelized leeks. Sprinkle cheese on top of leeks. Season generously with salt and pepper. Bake in oven about 1 hour, until potatoes are soft when tested with a fork. Remove from oven and let rest about 5 minutes before cutting.

Also known as lotte, angler fish, or belly fish, monkfish is said to be one of the ugliest fish there is. It is also one of the most aggressive predators. There is what looks like a fishing lure coming out of the top of its head, and that is how monkfish entice their prey; they sit on the ocean floor and wave their lure around, then bam!—they snap up their prey. Monkfish is found off the Atlantic Coast from the tip of South America to the northern parts of Canada. It is sold as tails rather than fillets because of its skeletal structure. It has a firm texture, similar to shrimp or lobster, and the meat is very rich. Oven roasting is a great way to prepare this fish.

MoNKFiSh

Portobello Reduction

Yield: 4 cups

Make this a day ahead. It is simple but time-consuming.

4 pounds veal bones	1 tablespoon peppercorns
2 cups chopped onion	2 bay leaves
5 cloves crushed garlic, plus 2 tablespoons minced	2 sprigs thyme, plus 2 tablespoons minced
1 quartered shallot, plus 2 tablespoons minced	2 sprigs oregano, plus 2 tablespoons minced
2 peeled and chopped carrots	1 gallon water
3 chopped celery stalks	3 diced portobello mushrooms
3 tablespoons tomato paste	Kosher salt
2 tablespoons olive oil	Freshly ground black pepper
1½ cups red wine	

Preheat oven to 350°F. Place bones in large roasting pan in oven for 60 minutes. Add onion, garlic cloves, quartered shallot, carrots, celery, and tomato paste to roasting pan. Place back in oven for another 30 minutes. Roast until bones and vegetables are slightly browned. Heat 1 tablespoon of olive oil in a large stockpot. Add roasted bones and vegetables. When they start to sizzle, deglaze with 1 cup of red wine and add peppercorns, bay leaves, and sprigs of thyme and oregano to the stockpot. Cover with water. Bring to a boil. Reduce heat and simmer for 8 hours. Let sit overnight in the refrigerator. Strain bones and vegetables out of stock and place liquid back in stockpot; reduce by half.

Place remaining tablespoon of olive oil in large sauté pan over high heat. When hot, add minced garlic and shallots and sauté until fragrant. Add mushrooms and cook until they release liquid and soften. Add minced thyme and oregano. Reduce heat slightly and cook until all liquid has evaporated from pan. Deglaze with remaining 1/2 cup red wine and let liquid evaporate from pan. Add mushroom mixture to reduced sauce. Season with salt and pepper.

Europeans introduced us to this abundant delicacy, which was first used as bait by American fisherman. Mussels are now very successfully farm raised on long ropes suspended from rafts in the Northeast Atlantic and Pacific Northwest. The majority of ours come from Prince Edward Island. They reach market size in less than a year, and the suspension method of growth ensures a much cleaner mussel, free of mud, sand, and grit. When you get them home from the store, your first job is to "debeard" the mussels. There is sometimes a black strand of byssus threads that hangs from the pointed end of the shell. Just pull down toward the pointed end of the mussel and it should come right off. To make sure the mussels are fresh and live, rinse with cold water and sort out any that have open shells. Gently tap the mussel on a hard surface and see if it closes. If it does, it is live and good to use; if not, discard. Mussels cook quickly, so be sure not to overcook them or they will get rubbery. They are great steamed or baked.

Mussels with Red Curry Cream

Yield: 4 servings

This also makes a great entrée for two over a pound of cooked linguini.

2	tablespoons red curry paste
3	tablespoons water
2	tablespoons olive oil
2	tablespoons minced garlic
2	tablespoons minced shallots
2	pounds debearded mussels
$\frac{1}{2}$	cup white wine
$\frac{1}{2}$	cup fish stock (p. 2)
$\frac{1}{2}$	cup heavy cream
1	tablespoon minced thyme
1	tablespoon minced oregano
1	tablespoon minced parsley
$\frac{1}{4}$	teaspoon kosher salt
$\frac{1}{8}$	teaspoon white pepper

Place curry paste in blender. Add water and blend until smooth in consistency. Place oil, garlic, shallots, and mussels in a large, heavy-bottom saucepan over high heat. Cook for 3 to 5 minutes until garlic is fragrant and pan is almost dry. Deglaze with white wine and add red curry slurry, fish stock, cream, thyme, oregano, parsley, salt, and pepper. Bring to a boil, then reduce heat slightly. Cover and cook 3 to 5 minutes, until all mussels are open.

 TO PLATE: *Pour into a large serving bowl and serve with some crusty bread.*

MuSSels

Mussel and Corn Chowda

Yield: 1/2 gallon

This recipe makes eight appetizer portions or four entrée portions of soup.

1 tablespoon olive oil

2 tablespoons minced garlic

2 tablespoons minced shallots

1 tablespoon minced thyme

1 tablespoon minced oregano

2 tablespoons minced parsley

1 pound rinsed and debearded mussels

1 cup white wine

2 cups fish stock (p. 2)

$\frac{1}{4}$ cup finely chopped bacon

1 cup finely diced onion

1 cup diced celery

1 cup corn kernels

$\frac{1}{2}$ cup finely diced red pepper

2 tablespoons butter

3 tablespoons flour

2 bay leaves

2 cups unpeeled, cooked, and diced red potatoes

1 cup heavy cream

1 teaspoon kosher salt

1 tablespoon black pepper

$\frac{1}{8}$ teaspoon cayenne

Freshly ground black pepper

TO COOK MUSSELS: Place oil in a 2-quart saucepan over high heat. Add garlic and shallots and sauté 2 to 3 minutes, until garlic is aromatic. Add thyme, oregano, 1 tablespoon of parsley, and mussels. Deglaze with white wine and then add fish stock. Bring to a boil, cover, and cook 3 to 5 minutes until all mussels are open. Remove from heat and cool. Drain and reserve mussel cooking liquid as stock. Remove mussels from shells and coarsely chop.

TO MAKE SOUP: Place bacon in a large stockpot over medium-high heat. Reduce heat to medium and let bacon render until crispy, 8 to 10 minutes. Add onion, celery, corn, and red pepper. Sauté until tender, approximately 8 to 10 minutes. Add butter and let melt. Add flour and stir to coat vegetables evenly. Let toast, stirring frequently for 12 to 15 minutes. Deglaze with reserved mussel stock. Add bay leaves, potatoes, cream, salt, black pepper, and cayenne. Bring to a boil. Reduce heat and let simmer for 30 minutes, until thickened. Add chopped mussels and cook a few minutes more.

TO PLATE: *Garnish with remaining minced parsley and freshly ground black pepper.*

Mussels with Ginger Aioli Salad

Yield: 8 servings

Mirin is Japanese rice wine. It is low in alcohol and has been slightly sweetened.

- 1 **tablespoon oil**
- 1 **tablespoon minced garlic**
- 1 **tablespoon minced shallots**
- 1 **tablespoon minced gingerroot**
- 4 **pounds rinsed and debearded mussels**
- $\frac{1}{2}$ **cup mirin**
- $\frac{1}{4}$ **cup water**
- 2 **cups rock salt**

Heat oil in a pot large enough to hold mussels comfortably with a cover. Add garlic, shallots, and ginger and sauté 2 to 3 minutes. Add mussels and deglaze with mirin, and then add water. Cover and bring to a boil. Reduce heat and simmer 3 to 4 minutes, until all mussels are open. Remove from heat. Pour off cooking liquid, cool, and reserve. Place mussels on a baking sheet and place in the refrigerator to cool. Remove the top shell from each mussel and loosen the meat from the other shell. Place shells with loosened mussel meat back on baking sheet that has been covered with half of the rock salt.

 TO PLATE: *Top mussels with Ginger Aioli Salad and transfer to serving dish that has been covered with remaining half of rock salt.*

TO MINCE GINGER: Peel ginger root and cut against the grain in 1/2-inch thick slices. Lay flat on cutting board and smash with the flat side of a French knife. This process will break apart the ginger making it easier and quicker to mince.

Ginger Aioli Salad

Yield: 1 1/3 cups

Pasteurized egg yolks should be available near whole eggs in your local supermarket.

- 2 **pasteurized egg yolks**
- 1 **tablespoon Chinese mustard**
- 1 **tablespoon minced gingerroot**
- 1 **tablespoon minced garlic**
- 1 **teaspoon rice wine vinegar**
- 2 **tablespoons reserved mussel cooking liquid**
- $\frac{1}{2}$ **cup sesame oil**
- $\frac{1}{2}$ **cup vegetable oil**
- 1 **peeled, seeded, and finely diced cucumber**
- 1 **bunch minced cilantro**
- 1 **finely diced red pepper**
- 1 **bunch minced green onions**
- $\frac{1}{4}$ **cup minced pickled ginger**
- 1 **peeled and finely diced carrot**
- **Kosher salt and white pepper**

Place egg yolks, mustard, minced ginger, garlic, vinegar, and reserved mussel cooking liquid in a food processor. Blend until yolks have thickened slightly and turned light yellow in color. With food processor running, add oils in a thin stream. The aioli mixture should end up the consistency of thin mayonnaise. Place cucumber, cilantro, red pepper, onions, pickled ginger, and carrot in a bowl. Toss with aioli. Season with salt and white pepper.

63

New Zealand Green-Lipped Mussels with Fennel and Pears

Yield: 4 servings

Any leftover fennel and pear topping is great over pasta.

- 1 **tablespoon olive oil**
- 2 **tablespoons minced garlic**
- 2 **tablespoons minced shallots**
- 2 **pounds rinsed and debearded New Zealand green-lipped mussels**
- 2 **tablespoons minced thyme**
- $\frac{1}{2}$ **teaspoon kosher salt**
- $\frac{1}{4}$ **teaspoon white pepper**
- $\frac{1}{4}$ **cup white wine**
- $\frac{1}{2}$ **cup water**
- 2 **cups rock salt**
- 2 **slices chopped bacon**
- 3 **stalks finely diced celery**
- 1 **finely diced fennel bulb**
- 1 **finely diced pear**
- 4 **tablespoons brandy**
- 1 **cup heavy cream**
- $\frac{1}{2}$ **cup grated Asiago cheese**

TO COOK MUSSELS: Place oil in saucepan over high heat. Add garlic and shallots and cook 3 to 4 minutes. Add mussels, thyme, salt, and pepper. Cook until almost all of the liquid has evaporated from the pan. Deglaze with white wine, then add water. Cover and let mussels steam 10 to 12 minutes, until the meat looks plump and firm. Remove from heat. Reserve cooking liquid as stock and let mussels cool. Line a baking sheet with 1 cup of rock salt. Remove top shell from mussel and discard. Loosen meat from bottom shell and place shell on baking sheet; this helps to keep the mussels from tipping over.

TO MAKE THE TOPPING: Preheat oven to 375°F. Place bacon in a small sauté pan and render until crispy. Add celery, fennel, and pear. Cook until soft, about 10 minutes. Deglaze with brandy, then add cream and reserved mussel cooking liquid. Cook until liquid reduces by half. Let cool slightly. Place a tablespoon of fennel and pear mixture onto each mussel half. Top with cheese. Bake for 10 to 15 minutes until hot and bubbly.

 TO PLATE: *Carefully transfer hot mussels to a large serving dish that has been covered with the remaining half of rock salt.*

New Zealand Green-Lipped Mussels

These shells can vary from black to brown, but the edges are always green. They are generally larger and meatier than the standard blue. The mature females turn an orange-apricot color. The closed, tight-shell rule does not apply to these mussels. As long as they smell fresh, they are fine to use. You still must remove the beards, though! They take a little longer to cook than the smaller blue mussels, but they are great steamed and baked.

Chipotle-Lime Marinated Opah with Vegetable Ragout, Shrimp and Sweet Potato Tamales

Yield: 4 servings

Chipotle chilies can be found canned in adobo sauce in the Mexican food section of your local grocery store. Just puree in the food processor; leftover puree can be kept in the freezer.

- $\frac{1}{4}$ cup olive oil
- 2 zested limes
- 1 juiced lime
- 4 tablespoons chipotle chili puree
- $\frac{1}{2}$ bunch minced cilantro
- $\frac{1}{2}$ teaspoon kosher salt
- $\frac{1}{8}$ teaspoon white pepper
- $1\frac{1}{2}$ pounds opah, cut into 4 pieces

Clean and oil surface of gas or charcoal grill, then preheat. In a large bowl, stir together oil, lime zest and juice, chili puree, cilantro, salt, and pepper until smooth. Place fillets in bowl, turn to coat evenly, and let marinate for 1 hour in refrigerator. Place fish on hot grill. Cook 3 minutes per side; cooking time may vary depending on thickness of fillet. Don't overcook this fish or it will be dry.

 TO PLATE: *Place a large spoonful of Vegetable Ragout onto each plate. Place fish on top of ragout and Hatch Salsa on top of fish. Cut Shrimp and Sweet Potato Tamales diagonally and place on edge of plates.*

This fish is also called moonfish. It is a large round fish like tuna and swordfish, sold in quarters. The raw fish is dark pink to red. The skin is pinkish gray and has white spots. The meat is very firm. It is easier to cook thin steaks because thicker pieces take longer to cook and can dry out easily.

oPaH

Vegetable Ragout

- 1 tablespoon olive oil
- 1 tablespoon minced garlic
- 1 tablespoon minced shallots
- 1 cup white beans, soaked in cold water overnight
- $\frac{1}{4}$ cup white wine
- 4 cups fish stock, plus more as needed (p. 2)
- 1 pint blanched and peeled pearl onions
- 1 pound cooked and halved baby purple potatoes
- 1 pint yellow cherry tomatoes
- 1 pint red cherry tomatoes
- 1 tablespoon minced thyme
- 1 tablespoon minced oregano
- 2 ounces diced butter
- Kosher salt
- Freshly ground black pepper

Place oil in large sauté pan over high heat. Add garlic and shallots and sauté 3 minutes. Add drained beans. Deglaze with wine, then add fish stock and bring to a boil. Reduce heat and simmer until beans are tender, 2 to 3 hours. Add more stock as necessary to keep beans covered in liquid. When beans are tender, add onions and potatoes and cook another 15 minutes; let liquid reduce to a stew consistency. Stir in tomatoes, thyme, oregano, and butter and simmer another 5 minutes. Season with salt and pepper.

Shrimp and Sweet Potato Tamales
Yield: 10 tamales

- ½ pound peeled and deveined small (31–40 ct) shrimp, shells reserved
- 1½ cups water
- 1 tablespoon olive oil
- 1 tablespoon minced garlic
- 1 tablespoon minced shallots
- Pinch kosher salt, plus 1/4 teaspoon
- Pinch white pepper
- 6 tablespoons (3/4 stick) room-temperature butter
- ¾ cup masa corn flour
- ¼ teaspoon baking powder
- 1 teaspoon honey
- Splash bourbon
- ⅔ cup cooked and diced sweet potatoes
- 15 corn husks soaked in warm water

TO MAKE SHRIMP STOCK: Place shrimp shells in a small pot with water and bring to a boil. Reduce heat and simmer 5 minutes. Strain shells from liquid; reserve liquid—this is your shrimp stock.

TO MAKE TAMALE FILLING: Place oil in small sauté pan over high heat. Add shrimp, garlic, shallots, pinch of salt and pepper, and sauté 2 to 3 minutes. Reduce heat and cook another 3 to 5 minutes.

Place butter and masa in a standing mixer with paddle attachment. Whip until coarse crumbs form. Add 1/2 cup warm shrimp stock. Whip until smooth and let rest 5 minutes. Add shrimp and all remaining ingredients. Mix together briefly; do not mash.

TO MAKE TAMALES: Tear several corn husks into strips to tie the ends of the tamales. Lay one husk out flat. Place 2 tablespoons of masa mixture in center of corn husk. Fold sides over filling, and tie ends with torn corn husk strips. Place tamales in top of steamer pan, cover, and cook for 20 minutes. Remove from heat and cover with warm wet towel; let rest 20 minutes.

Hatch Salsa
Yield: 1 1/2 cups

- 2 large Roma tomatoes
- 2 large tomatillos, husks removed
- ½ jalapeño
- ¼ small onion
- 1 tablespoon olive oil
- Kosher salt
- Freshly ground black pepper
- 1 tablespoon balsamic vinegar
- 1 tablespoon red wine vinegar
- 2 tablespoons lime juice
- ¼ bunch minced cilantro
- ½ cup canned diced green chilies

Clean and oil surface of gas or charcoal grill, then preheat. Place tomatoes, tomatillos, jalapeño, and onion in a bowl and toss with oil. Season with salt and pepper. Place vegetables on hot grill. Cook on all sides until slightly blackened and softened. Remove from grill and cool. Coarsely chop all vegetables. Place vegetables and rest of ingredients in a food processor and pulse until smooth. Add salt and pepper to taste. Refrigerate until ready to use.

Oysters can be compared to wine in that their quality and flavor is dependent on water, temperature, currents, storms, coastal soils, and salt, mineral, and algae content in the tides—all sorts of uncontrollable environmental factors. They are filter feeders, so they literally are what they eat. They feed on tiny one-celled organisms called diatoms, which are very high in minerals, and they are named by the geographic location they are grown in (for example, a bay), not by species.

OYSTERS

TO SHUCK OYSTERS: Fold an old kitchen towel in thirds lengthwise and lay flat on work surface. Place oyster in center of towel, with rounded end pointing toward the left end of towel. Fold that end of towel over oyster. Place your left hand on top of oyster and fold towel back over your hand. This will hold the oyster firmly in place and protect your hand from the oyster knife. Pick up the oyster knife with your right hand. Wedge the tip of the oyster knife into the hinge of the oyster. This will be found where the two shells are attached together at the pointed end of the oyster. Pry oyster open with a twist of the knife. Slide oyster knife along top edge, inside the shell, and remove. Slide oyster knife along bottom inside shell to loosen meat. Be careful not to spill oyster liquor (the liquid found in the shell).

Southeastern—These pungent oysters are characterized by their creamy, earthy-tasting flesh that stems from the bays they live and feed in. The Apalachicola oysters, from the bay by the same name in northwest Florida, an inlet of the Gulf of Mexico, typifies the southeastern oyster. Although great when eaten raw, their brackish flavor and their durability make them excellent additions to stews and casseroles and baked or broiled dishes.

Northeastern—Characteristically salty and crisp, these coastal delicacies are made for raw consumption. A thick, shallow shell provides protection from the harsh northern elements. Inside lies a translucent gem-like flesh that dissolves in your mouth. These oysters are best eaten raw.

Pacific Northwest—Spawned in the tranquil sounds of Washington and Oregon, these thin-shelled, deep-cupped oysters are delicate and succulent. Typically very creamy, meaty, and low in salt, they possess a melon-like aftertaste. Because of their plump size and milky consistency, these oysters are great when either cooked or eaten raw.

British Columbia—This vast area of coastline produces some amazing oysters. Fed by mineral-rich glacial melt, these oysters are deep cupped and have a metallic to cucumber aftertaste. Although similar to the Pacific Northwest oysters, their taste is significantly stronger. It is this flavor that makes B.C. oysters outstanding with decadent accouterments.

Oysters Bienville

Yield: 1 1/2 cups, 6 servings

- $\frac{1}{4}$ cup finely diced bacon
- $\frac{1}{2}$ tablespoon JAX Blackening Spice
- 1 tablespoon minced garlic
- 2 tablespoons minced shallots
- $\frac{1}{2}$ tablespoon minced thyme
- $\frac{1}{2}$ tablespoon minced oregano
- $\frac{1}{2}$ tablespoon minced parsley, plus 1/4 cup chopped for garnish
- 2 cups sliced crimini mushrooms
- $\frac{1}{2}$ cup finely diced red pepper
- 1 tablespoon butter
- 2 tablespoons flour
- $\frac{1}{4}$ cup brandy
- $\frac{1}{2}$ cup heavy cream
- 8 ounces (1 cup) peeled and deveined rock shrimp
- $\frac{1}{4}$ teaspoon kosher salt
- $\frac{1}{8}$ teaspoon freshly ground black pepper
- 2 cups rock salt
- 2 dozen shucked East Coast oysters on the half shell
- $\frac{1}{2}$ cup grated Asiago cheese

Preheat oven to 400°F. Place bacon in a large sauté pan over high heat and render until crispy. Add JAX Blackening Spice, garlic, shallots, thyme, oregano, and 1/2 tablespoon of parsley. Sauté another 2 minutes, stirring frequently until garlic is fragrant and spices are toasted. Add mushrooms and red pepper. Cook until mushrooms have released their liquid and pan is almost dry. Add butter and let melt. Add flour and stir to coat; let flour toast for 12 to 15 minutes (it should start to smell nutty), stirring frequently to avoid burning.

Deglaze with brandy and add cream. Bring to a boil. Reduce heat and let simmer until reduced by one quarter and thickened. Add shrimp, kosher salt, and pepper and cook 3 minutes more, until shrimp are cooked through. Spread half of the rock salt on cookie sheet. Place oysters on the half shell on the rock salt. Be careful not to spill the oyster liquor. Place a tablespoon of mushroom mixture on top of each oyster. Sprinkle with cheese. Set in oven and bake until hot and bubbly, about 15 minutes.

 TO PLATE: *Carefully transfer hot oysters to a serving platter that has been covered with remaining rock salt and garnish with chopped parsley.*

70

Russian Oysters

Yield: 2 servings

Remember—these are raw so keep them cold. We suggest Kushi or Sinku oysters for this dish—something from the Pacific Northwest.

- **1 cup crushed ice or rock salt**
- **12 of your favorite oysters from the Pacific Northwest**
- **1½ teaspoons crème fraîche (p. 2)**
- **¼ ounce of your favorite caviar**

Arrange crushed ice or rock salt on a serving dish. Shuck oysters (for instructions, see page 69), reserving as much liquor as possible and place on the half shell, on ice. Place a small dollop, 1/8 teaspoon, of crème fraîche on top of the oyster. Place a knife tip of caviar on top of crème fraîche. Serve immediately!

72

Dispelling the "R" Month Myth

Don't eat oysters in May, June, July, and August because they aren't as good as in the winter. Yeah, right. This is the new millennium baby—you can eat oysters whenever you want. In fact, you can get almost anything you want anytime you want it.

There is this new thing called the global economy that helps us to get oysters from other cold waters (like New Zealand) in our summer months. There are also ways to stagger different oyster beds' growing seasons so they don't all spawn at once. After all, the water never gets very warm in British Columbia. So don't be afraid to dive right in—there are plenty of fabulous oysters available every day of the year.

Blood Orange Ginger Marmalade

Yield: 4 cups

Be sure to use a large pot when making this marmalade because when you boil the sugar, it will foam up.

- **4 blood oranges**
- **1 lemon**
- **4 tablespoons minced gingerroot**
- **½ teaspoon red pepper flakes**
- **1½ cups water**
- **⅛ teaspoon baking soda**
- **1 ounce (1/2 box or 2 tablespoons) fruit pectin**
- **5 cups sugar**
- **2 tablespoons horseradish for garnish**

Sterilize glass jars and lids. Zest oranges and lemon and place zest in a large (4- to 6-quart) pot with ginger, red pepper flakes, water, and baking soda. Bring to a boil. Reduce heat and simmer 10 minutes. Meanwhile, section the oranges and lemon by first cutting off the top and bottom. With a sharp paring knife, cut the peel from the fruit, being sure to remove all the bitter white pith. Next, remove wedges of fruit from between tough membrane sections, remove seeds, and squeeze leftover membrane to get every last bit of juice. Add fruit pulp and juice to pot and simmer another 10 minutes. Add pectin. Bring to a boil and cook 1 minute. Slowly stir in sugar and bring to a rolling boil. Boil for 10 minutes, then pour mixture into sterilized jars and let sit overnight.

 TO PLATE: *Place a teaspoon of marmalade on top of a freshly shucked oyster with a little extra horseradish—yum!*

Cranberry Horseradish Marmalade

Yield: 4 cups

Use a large pot when making this recipe because when you boil the sugar, it will foam up.

- **6 ounces (1 cup) dried cranberries**
- **1 zested and sectioned lemon**
- **2 cups water**
- **1/8 teaspoon baking soda**
- **1 ounce (1/2 box or 2 tablespoons) fruit pectin**
- **4 cups sugar**
- **2 tablespoons horseradish, plus more for garnish**

Sterilize jars and lids. Combine cranberries, lemon zest and sections, water, and baking soda in a large (4- to 6-quart) saucepot. Bring to a boil. Reduce heat and simmer 10 minutes. Add pectin and bring to a boil. Cook 1 minute. Slowly stir in sugar and bring back to a rolling boil. Cook for 10 minutes. Stir in horseradish and let boil 1 more minute. Pour into sterilized jars and let sit overnight.

 TO PLATE: *Place a teaspoon on top of a freshly shucked oyster with a little extra horseradish.*

Frozen Bloody Mary Mignonette

Yield: 3/4 cup, 12 servings

In French kitchens, *mignonette* means "crushed pepper"; in U.S. oyster bars it means a peppery sauce made with shallots and vinegar served on top of raw oysters.

These mixtures will not freeze completely because of the alcohol in it, and it will separate into layers. You will need to break it up with a mixing spoon and stir back together before serving.

- **1/4 cup JAX Bloody Mary Mix (p. 26)**
- **2 tablespoons your favorite vodka**
- **2 tablespoons red wine vinegar**
- **2 tablespoons rice wine vinegar**
- **2 tablespoons finely chopped shallots**

Whisk all ingredients together and place in freezer overnight. Serve 1 tablespoon of mignonette on top of a freshly shucked oyster.

Frozen Champagne Mignonette

Yield: 1 1/2 cups, 24 servings

- **1/2 split (half) bottle of champagne**
- **1/4 cup rice wine vinegar**
- **1/4 cup red wine vinegar**
- **1/4 cup finely minced shallots**
- **2 tablespoons crushed pink peppercorns**

Whisk all ingredients together and place in the freezer overnight. Serve 1 tablespoon of mignonette on top of a freshly shucked oyster.

Red Snapper en Papillote with Spring Vegetables

Yield: 4 servings

If you cannot find a large piece of parchment paper, tin foil will work. Pastis is an anise-flavored liqueur from the south of France.

> 2   artichokes
>
> 1   bunch trimmed asparagus
>
> 4   peeled pencil-thin carrots
>
> 4   quartered sunburst squash
>
>   Olive oil
>
>   Kosher salt for seasoning, plus 1/2 teaspoon
>
>   White pepper for seasoning, plus 1/4 teaspoon
>
> 1   thinly sliced fennel bulb
>
> $1\frac{1}{2}$ pounds whole red snapper, head removed
>
> $\frac{1}{4}$ cup pastis
>
> 1   cup basmati rice
>
> 2   cups fish stock (p. 2)
>
> 1   cup beurre blanc (p. 1)

Preheat oven to 375°F. Place a large piece of parchment paper or foil in a roasting pan. Quarter artichokes and scoop out the fuzz. Cut asparagus into thirds. Cut carrots into 2-inch-long sticks. Place squash, artichokes, asparagus, and carrots in roasting pan and drizzle with olive oil. Season with salt and white pepper. Place fennel inside the fish cavity and season fish with olive oil, salt, and pepper. Lay fish on top of vegetables. Pour pastis over fish.

Wrap parchment up around vegetables and fish. Fold over or staple shut so that the steam cannot escape the parchment. Roast in the oven for 1 hour and 30 minutes. Vegetables should be tender and fish cooked through. Meanwhile, combine the rice and stock in a sauté pan and bring to a boil. Add 1/2 teaspoon salt and 1/4 teaspoon pepper. Reduce heat, cover, and simmer until water is absorbed and rice is cooked—20 minutes. Make beurre blanc.

 TO PLATE: *Cut parchment paper open with scissors or a knife, then remove fish to a cutting board to fillet. The meat should slide easily from the bone. Score meat above backbone and slide knife edge down toward the belly of the fish, being careful not to cut through the small pin bones. Turn fish over and do the same on the other side. Cut the two fillets in half. Place a large scoop of rice in the center of each plate. Surround the rice with steamed vegetables, and place a piece of fish on top of rice. Drizzle with beurre blanc.*

There are approximately 250 species of snapper, fifteen of which are found in U.S. waters. Silkie snapper is also called red snapper, rouget, or Mexican snapper. Snappers are warm-water fish, and they live in deep-water reefs. They are small fish, usually one to three pounds, and sometimes come whole and gutted but need to be scaled—make sure they do that at the grocery store for you! They also come in fillet form. Occasionally something will be labeled snapper that is actually rockfish, which is entirely different than snapper; be leery if the red skin has been taken off. Snappers are great to grill or roast if they are whole. If you get fillets, it is better to pan roast them.

red snapper

Pan-Seared Red Snapper over Barley Salad with Cucumber Dill Cream

Yield: 4 servings

Tamari is a slightly thicker and lower in salt than regular soy sauce.

- 6 tablespoons olive oil
- 1 cup diced onion
- 2 tablespoons minced garlic
- 2 tablespoons minced shallots
- 1 cup pearl barley
- 4 cups fish stock (p. 2)
- 2 sprigs oregano
- 1 pint cherry tomatoes
- 1 pound green beans
- 3 tablespoons sherry vinegar
  Kosher salt and white pepper
- 1 tablespoon tamari
- $1\frac{1}{2}$ pounds red snapper fillets, cut into 4 equal pieces
- 2 tablespoons minced mint
  Sweet soy sauce

Preheat oven to 400°F. Place 1 tablespoon of the oil in a medium saucepan over high heat. Add onion and sauté until translucent, 8 to 10 minutes. Add garlic and shallots. Cook another 2 minutes and add barley. Deglaze with fish stock. Add oregano and bring to a boil. Reduce heat to simmer and cook 35 to 45 minutes, until all liquid has been absorbed and barley is tender. Meanwhile, cut cherry tomatoes into quarters and blanch green beans for 3 minutes in boiling water until bright green and just tender. Season tomatoes with 1 tablespoon of vinegar, 1 tablespoon of oil, and salt and pepper to taste. Season green beans with 1 tablespoon of oil, salt, and pepper. (Do not season green beans with sherry vinegar or they will loose their bright green color.)

Let barley cool slightly and then add 2 tablespoons of oil, 2 remaining tablespoons of vinegar, and tamari. Add salt and pepper to taste. Place remaining tablespoon of olive oil in a large oven-safe sauté pan over high heat. Season snapper with salt, pepper, and mint. When pan is hot, add snapper and let pan sear for 2 to 3 minutes, until golden brown. Turn fish over and place pan in oven to finish cooking another 3 to 4 minutes.

 TO PLATE: *Pour 1/3 cup (roughly 3 ounces) of Cucumber Dill Cream sauce onto each plate and swirl to coat base. Place a small pile of green beans in the center of the plate and top with a scoop of Barley Salad. Divide cherry tomatoes among plates and arrange in sauce. Top Barley Salad with fish and drizzle with sweet soy sauce.*

Cucumber Dill Cream

Yield: 1 3/4 cups

- 2 large cucumbers
- 2 tablespoons minced dill
- $1\frac{1}{2}$ tablespoons fresh lemon juice
- $\frac{1}{3}$ cup heavy cream
- $\frac{1}{2}$ teaspoon kosher salt
- $\frac{1}{8}$ teaspoon white pepper

Peel, seed, and coarsely chop cucumbers and place in a blender with remaining ingredients. Puree just until smooth, being sure not to overprocess or cream will become too thick to pour.

These fish are caught in both the Atlantic and Pacific Oceans. There are five species of Pacific salmon. Chinook (king) salmon mature in four years and grow to between fifteen and thirty pounds. Chum (dog or keta) salmon mature in three to six years and grow to between eight and twelve pounds. Coho (silver or jack) salmon are about four to sixteen pounds and take about three to five years to mature. Pink (humpback) salmon are the smallest and most abundant, and in two years they grow to six pounds; this species doesn't swim upstream to spawn—they just spawn at the high tide line. Sockeye (red or blueback) salmon mature in four years and are about seven pounds. Due to high demand, Atlantic salmon have been very successfully farm raised in Chile. The farm-raised salmon are lighter pink in color (the wild can get to be a deep shade of red), less gamey in flavor, and lower in fat content than their wild counterparts. Spring through summer is when salmon head upstream to spawn, so occasionally a wild species will be available in the supermarket, like Copper River salmon. If there is a specific area named where the fish is being sold, it is probably wild. The predominant times to find wild salmon in your grocery store are from May through September. Atlantic salmon can run upstream to spawn several times, whereas Pacific salmon spawn only once then die. Salmon is a very versatile fish and is great on the grill, pan seared, or oven roasted.

sAlmOn

Smoked Salmon Platter with Three-Radish Potato Salad and Mustard Sauce

Yield: 4 servings

- 4 slices bread
- 3 tablespoons olive oil
- 1 black radish
- $\frac{1}{2}$ bunch thinly sliced red radishes
- 2 pounds cooked and diced baby red potatoes
- $\frac{1}{2}$ cup mayonnaise
- 1 tablespoon Dijon mustard
- 2 teaspoons horseradish
- $\frac{1}{2}$ teaspoon kosher salt
- $\frac{1}{8}$ teaspoon white pepper
- 8 ounces smoked salmon
- 2 quartered hard-boiled eggs
- $\frac{1}{2}$ cup niçoise olives
- $\frac{1}{4}$ cup brunoise red onion
- $\frac{1}{3}$ cup capers

TO MAKE CROSTINI: Preheat oven to 400°F. Cut crust off from bread and brush bread with olive oil. Cut in half diagonally both ways so you have 4 triangles. Place triangles on a baking sheet and toast in oven until crispy.

TO MAKE THREE-RADISH POTATO SALAD: Peel black radish and cut into julienne strips (matchstick-size pieces). Place in a bowl with red radishes, potatoes, mayonnaise, mustard, horseradish, salt, and pepper. Combine thoroughly.

Mustard Sauce

Yield: 3/4 cup, 5 servings

- 1 tablespoon dry mustard
- $\frac{1}{2}$ cup mayonnaise
- 1$\frac{1}{2}$ tablespoons Worcestershire sauce
- 1 tablespoon A-1 Steak Sauce
- 1$\frac{1}{2}$ tablespoons heavy cream
- Kosher salt and white pepper

Place all ingredients in a small bowl and whisk together until smooth. Pour into a squeeze tube.

77

 TO PLATE: *Place large mound of potato salad in the center of a serving platter. Fan strips of smoked salmon out over one side of the plate slightly overlapping each other and halfway up potato salad. On the other side of the plate, stick crostini into potato salad in a fan shape. Garnish smoked salmon plate with sliced eggs, olives, onion, and capers. Then drizzle entire platter with Mustard Sauce.*

Smoked Salmon Caesar Salad

Yield: 2 cups dressing, 8 servings of salad

Cholula is a hot sauce, similar to Tabasco. You can buy it online at cholula.com.

- 2 pasteurized egg yolks
- 2 tablespoons minced garlic
- 2 tablespoons red wine vinegar
- 2 tablespoons lemon juice
- 1 tablespoon Worcestershire sauce
- 1 tablespoon Dijon mustard
- 1 dash Cholula
- $\frac{1}{4}$ teaspoon white pepper
- $\frac{1}{2}$ teaspoon kosher salt
- $1\frac{1}{2}$ cups olive oil
- $\frac{1}{4}$ cup chopped anchovies
- 6 heads romaine heart leaves
- 8 ounces smoked salmon
- $\frac{1}{2}$ cup grated Asiago cheese
- Freshly ground black pepper

Place first nine ingredients in a large bowl or food processor. Whisk or pulse until smooth and pale yellow in color. Slowly incorporate oil in a thin stream until thickened. Stir in anchovies. Place whole, washed, and dried romaine heart leaves in another bowl. Ladle approximately 2/3 cup (roughly 6 ounces), a little less than half, of dressing onto leaves and toss to coat evenly. Add more dressing, to taste, if necessary. Remember, you can always add more but you can never take it out!

 TO PLATE: *Arrange dressed leaves on individual plates (oval-shaped work well) with stem ends together. Garnish with salmon, cheese, and black pepper.*

Smoked Salmon Niçoise San

Yield: 2 servings

If you can't find Russian black bread, pumpernickel will do.

- 1 large Idaho potato
- 4 slices Russian black bread
- $\frac{1}{4}$ cup Kalamata Olive Aioli
- 2 cups arugula
- 2 sliced hard-boiled eggs
- $\frac{1}{4}$ thinly sliced red onion
- $\frac{1}{4}$ pound thinly sliced smoked salmon

Clean and oil surface of gas or charcoal grill, then preheat. Peel potato and slice into 1/4-inch-thick pieces. Blanch in boiling water until tender. Season potato slices with oil and grill for 2 to 3 minutes per side. Toast slices of black bread. Slather with Kalamata Olive Aioli. Layer arugula, hard-boiled egg, onion, salmon, and grilled potatoes between slices of bread.

 TO PLATE: *Cut sandwich in half and serve with JAX Chips (page 50).*

wich with Kalamata Olive Aioli and JAX Chips

Kalamata Olive Aioli
Yield: 1 1/4 cups

- $\frac{1}{3}$ cup pitted kalamata olives
- 1 pasteurized egg yolk
- 1 tablespoon roasted garlic (p. 3)
- 3 baked and juiced lemons (p. 106)
- $\frac{1}{4}$ teaspoon kosher salt
- $\frac{1}{8}$ teaspoon white pepper
- 1 cup olive oil

Place olives in food processor and puree until smooth. Add egg yolk, garlic, lemon juice, salt, and pepper. Process for 3 to 4 minutes, until slightly thickened. With the food processor running, slowly add oil in a thin stream.

Carbonara

Yield: 4 servings

The pancetta and mushrooms are cooked ahead of time to make sure the sauce remains creamy white. Be sure to add the smoked salmon at the very end so it doesn't cook through.

- 2 tablespoons olive oil
- 2 tablespoons minced garlic
- 2 tablespoons minced shallots
- $\frac{1}{4}$ cup finely chopped rendered pancetta
- $\frac{1}{2}$ cup white wine
- $\frac{1}{2}$ cup fish stock (p. 2)
- 1 cup heavy cream
- 1 pound cooked mafaldina pasta
- 2 cups sliced and cooked crimini mushrooms
- 1 cup grated Asiago cheese
- 1 tablespoon minced thyme
- 1 tablespoon minced oregano
- 1 tablespoon minced parsley
- $\frac{1}{2}$ teaspoon kosher salt
- $\frac{1}{4}$ pound finely chopped smoked salmon
- Freshly ground black pepper

Heat olive oil in large sauté pan over medium-high heat. Add garlic, shallots, and pancetta. Sauté 2 to 3 minutes, until garlic is fragrant. Deglaze with wine and add fish stock and cream. Let sauce come to a boil and reduce sauce until slightly thickened, 2 to 3 minutes. Add pasta, mushrooms, 1/2 cup of cheese, thyme, oregano, parsley, and salt. Bring back to a boil and let ingredients heat through.

 TO PLATE: *Divide pasta among four individual serving bowls. Garnish with remaining 1/2 cup of cheese, salmon, and pepper.*

TO RENDER PANCETTA: Preheat oven to 325°F. Arrange slices on a baking sheet and bake in oven until crispy, about 1 hour. Let cool slightly and place in a colander to drain off fat.

TO COOK CRIMINIS: Place 1 tablespoon of olive oil in a hot sauté pan. Add mushrooms and cook until mushrooms soften and release liquid; continue cooking until pan is almost dry.

Grilled Salmon with Cilantro Basmati Rice, Miso Ginger Broth, and Cucumber Salad

Yield: 6

Basmati rice is a long-grain, fragrant rice used in Indian and Middle Eastern cooking.

2 cups basmati rice	$\frac{1}{2}$ teaspoon kosher salt, plus more for seasoning
4 cups fish stock (p. 2)	$\frac{1}{4}$ teaspoon white pepper, plus more for seasoning
2 tablespoons minced cilantro	$2\frac{1}{4}$ pounds salmon, cut into 6 equal pieces
1 tablespoon minced parsley	1 tablespoon olive oil

Clean and oil surface of gas or charcoal grill, then preheat. Place rice, fish stock, 1 tablespoon cilantro, parsley, 1/2 teaspoon salt, and 1/4 teaspoon pepper in a medium-size saucepan over high heat. Bring to a boil. Reduce heat to low and cover and simmer approximately 30 minutes, until rice is tender. Season salmon fillets with oil, remaining 1 tablespoon cilantro, and salt and pepper to taste. Place salmon on hot grill. Cook 3 minutes per side depending on thickness of fish and desired cooking temperature.

 TO PLATE: *Ladle 3/4 cup (6 ounces) of Miso Ginger Broth into six shallow bowls. Place a large scoop of rice in the center of each bowl. Place the salmon on top of the rice. Place the Cucumber Salad on top of the salmon and serve!*

Miso Ginger Broth

Yield: 6 cups

Miso is fermented soybean paste. It is found in some grocery stores and most Asian markets.

1 tablespoon vegetable oil	1 julienne red pepper (2-inch-long pieces)
1 tablespoon minced garlic	$\frac{1}{2}$ cup white wine
2 tablespoons minced shallots	4 cups fish stock (p. 2)
$\frac{1}{2}$ cup minced gingerroot	$\frac{1}{2}$ cup white miso paste
1 julienne leek (2-inch-long pieces)	$\frac{1}{2}$ cup soy sauce
2 julienne celery stalks (2-inch-long pieces)	3 tablespoons minced parsley
2 julienne carrots (2-inch-long pieces)	1 bunch diagonally sliced green onions

Place oil, garlic, shallots, and ginger in a large sauté pan over medium-high heat. Sauté until fragrant, 3 to 5 minutes. Add leeks, celery, carrots, and red pepper. Cook 10 to 12 minutes, until softened and slightly caramelized. Deglaze with wine. Add fish stock and bring to a boil. Reduce heat and simmer 5 minutes. Whisk together miso paste and soy sauce; slowly whisk into vegetable broth. Simmer another 5 minutes. Add parsley and green onions and turn off heat. This broth should not be cooked a long time. If you want to make it ahead of time, turn off the heat and bring back to a boil just before serving.

TO TOAST SESAME SEEDS: Place on a baking sheet in 350°F oven for 6 to 8 minutes, or until fragrant.

Cucumber Salad

Yield: 1 1/2 cups

2 **peeled cucumbers**

3 **tablespoons toasted black sesame seeds**

1 **tablespoon sesame oil**

1 **teaspoon kosher salt**

1 **teaspoon sugar**

2 **tablespoons rice wine vinegar**

Cut cucumbers in half lengthwise, scoop out seeds, and slice at an angle as thinly as possible. Place in a small bowl and toss with remaining ingredients. Make this as close to serving time as possible so cucumbers stay crisp.

SALMON

Pecan-Crusted Salmon with Red Chard and Wild Rice Chowda

Yield: 4 servings

- $\frac{1}{2}$ cup toasted and finely chopped pecans
- 2 tablespoons flour
- 1 tablespoon minced garlic
- $\frac{1}{2}$ teaspoon kosher salt
- $\frac{1}{4}$ teaspoon white pepper
- 2 tablespoons olive oil
- $1\frac{1}{2}$ pounds salmon, cut into 4 equal portions
- 1 large bunch coarsely chopped red chard leaves
- 1 tablespoon bourbon

Preheat oven to 400°F.

In a small bowl, toss together pecans, flour, garlic, salt, and pepper.

Press salmon fillets into pecan crust. Heat oil in an oven-safe sauté pan over medium-high heat. Set salmon fillets crust side down in pan. Be careful not to get the pan too hot or you will burn the pecans. Let salmon sear 2 to 3 minutes, until pecans are golden brown. Turn over and place in oven to finish roasting, 4 to 5 minutes more.

Meanwhile, place the remaining tablespoon of oil in another sauté pan over high heat. Add red chard and turn briefly to wilt. Deglaze with bourbon and keep turning until evenly wilted.

TO PLATE: *Ladle 1/3 cup (roughly 3 ounces) of Wild Rice Chowda onto each plate. Place a large mound of red chard in the center of the plate. Place fish on top of chard. Garnish each plate with 4 reserved mussels from Wild Rice Chowda recipe.*

Wild Rice Chowda

Yield: 7 cups

- 1 tablespoon olive oil
- 1 tablespoon minced garlic
- 1 tablespoon minced shallots
- 2 pounds rinsed and debearded mussels
- $\frac{1}{4}$ cup white wine
- 2 sprigs thyme
- 2 sprigs oregano
- 4 cups fish stock (p. 2)
- $\frac{1}{4}$ cup diced bacon
- 1 cup diced onion
- 1 cup diced celery
- 1 cup peeled and diced carrots
- 1 small diced red pepper
- 4 tablespoons (1/2 stick) butter
- 4 tablespoons flour
- 2 cups water
- 1 cup wild rice
- $\frac{1}{2}$ cup heavy cream

TO MAKE MUSSEL LIQUOR: Place oil in a pot (large enough to hold and cover mussels) over high heat. Add garlic and shallots and sauté until fragrant, 2 to 3 minutes. Add mussels and deglaze with wine. Add thyme, oregano, and fish stock. Cover and let cook 4 minutes, until mussels appear plump and shells are open. Drain and reserve cooking liquid—this is your mussel liquor. Reserve 16 whole mussels to garnish Pecan-Crusted Salmon plate. Remove the meat from remaining shells. Coarsely chop and reserve to add to chowder.

TO MAKE CHOWDA: Place bacon in a large saucepot over high heat and render until crispy. Add onion, celery, carrots, and red pepper and sauté until translucent, 10 to 15 minutes. Reduce heat to low. Add butter and melt. Add flour and toast, stirring frequently for 10 more minutes. Return heat to high. Deglaze with mussel cooking liquor and add water, rice, and cream. Bring to a boil. Reduce heat to a simmer and cook for 45 minutes to 1 hour until rice is tender and soup has thickened. Add reserved chopped mussel meat and heat through.

Calico Bay Scallop and Pineapple Ceviche

Yield: 4 servings

The scallops need to marinate a couple of hours before serving. The lime juice changes the protein structure of the scallops, so it looks "cooked."

- 1 **pound bay scallops**
- 3 **zested and juiced limes**
- 1 **zested and juiced lemon**
- 1 **seeded and finely diced jalapeño**
- 1 **cup diced pineapple**
- ½ **bunch minced cilantro**
- 1 **tablespoon sesame seeds**
- 1 **bunch finely chopped green onions**
- 2 **tablespoons sesame oil**
- ½ **teaspoon kosher salt, plus more for seasoning**
- ¼ **teaspoon white pepper, plus more for seasoning**
  Oil for fryer
- 4 **egg roll skins**

Mix all ingredients together except egg roll skins, and let marinate in the refrigerator for 2 hours; scallops should turn opaque. Preheat fryer to 350°F. Cut egg roll skins in half and then cut rectangles in half diagonally to form long triangles. Place egg roll skins in hot oil and fry until crisp and golden. Season with salt and pepper.

 TO PLATE: *Place Pineapple Ceviche in martini glasses and stick 3 or 4 egg roll skin triangles in the center of the ceviche, pointed end down.*

84

There are three varieties of scallops. From largest to smallest, they are sea, bay, and calico. Sea scallops are harvested off the coasts of Maine, southern New England, and the mid-Atlantic states; they are approximately 10 units to a pound (U10). Bay scallops are generally caught off the coasts of Long Island and Massachusetts and are 50–90 count per pound. Calicos thrive in warmer water off the coasts of Florida and are as small as 70–200 count per pound. Scallops live on the sea bottom and must be hand picked by divers. They live near currents and are filter feeders that swim by jet propulsion. They can see shadows through dotlike eyes that ring the mantel of the shell, complete with lens, optic nerve, cornea, and retina. To use scallops after you get them home from the store, they should just be rinsed and the "foot" removed. There is a tiny white opaque muscle that adheres to the side of the scallop, which can be pulled off gently with your fingers.

sCaLloPs

Coquilles St. JAX

Yield: 6 servings

3   pounds large (U10 ct) scallops
     (about 4 or 5 per person)

4   pounds peeled and chopped Idaho potatoes

4   tablespoons (1/2 stick) butter

$1\frac{1}{2}$ cups half-and-half

2   tablespoons roasted garlic (p. 3)

$\frac{1}{2}$ teaspoon kosher salt, plus more for seasoning

$\frac{1}{4}$ teaspoon white pepper, plus more for seasoning

1   bunch trimmed asparagus

1   tablespoon roasted garlic oil (p. 3)

2   tablespoons minced garlic

2   tablespoons minced shallots

2   bay leaves

$\frac{1}{2}$ cup white wine

$\frac{1}{2}$ cup fish stock (p. 2)

2   tablespoons chiffonade sage leaves

$\frac{2}{3}$ cup brown butter

86

TO PLATE: *Spoon a large mound of mashed potatoes onto the center of each plate. Divide asparagus among plates, and lean tips straight up the mound of mashed potatoes. Arrange scallops around front edge of plate. Divide scallop pan sauce evenly among plates.*

Rinse and drain scallops. Remove small white muscle on the curved edge of scallop. Pat scallops dry. If they are very wet, place them in a strainer and let liquid drain off for 30 minutes or so. If they are still wet, dust them with a little flour, for better searing.

Place potatoes in large pot of water and bring to a boil. Reduce heat to simmer and let potatoes cook until fork-tender. Place potatoes through a food mill or hand mash. Melt butter in small saucepan. Add half-and-half, roasted garlic, 1/2 teaspoon salt, and 1/4 teaspoon pepper. Bring to a boil. Mix a little at a time into mashed potatoes until moist, but still stiff. Keep warm.

Heat a sauté pan over medium-high heat. Bring a pot of water to a boil and blanch asparagus. Meanwhile, in a dry, smokin' hot pan, add scallops, flat side down, and sear on one side. Season with salt and pepper. Let cook 2 to 3 minutes, then turn scallops over. Add oil, minced garlic, shallots, and bay leaves. Cook another 2 to 3 minutes, until garlic is fragrant. Be careful not to burn garlic—you may have to reduce the heat. Deglaze with wine, then add fish stock and sage. Bring to a boil and let liquid reduce by half. Add brown butter, swirl pan to release scallops and incorporate butter.

TO BROWN BUTTER: Place 1/2 pound (2 sticks) of butter in a small saucepan over medium heat and melt. As butter continues to sit over heat, solids will start to caramelize and sink to the bottom of pan. Skim surface of butter with ladle to remove any foam. Liquid in pan will eventually turn brown in color and clear. Remove pan from heat. Pour melted butter fat into another heat-proof container, being careful not to pour in browned bits in the bottom of the pan. This process takes about 30 minutes.

Tarragon-Crusted Scallops with Absolut Citron Yellow Tomato Sauce and Tarragon Oil

Yield: 4 servings

3   roughly chopped yellow tomatoes

½   cup water

1   roughly chopped yellow pepper

1   tablespoon olive oil

1   tablespoon minced shallots

1   tablespoon roasted garlic (p. 3)

1   tablespoon minced thyme

1   tablespoon minced oregano

1   ounce Absolut Citron Vodka

¼   cup heavy cream

½   cup frozen peas

    Kosher salt and white pepper

1   pound linguine

2   pounds large (U10 ct) scallops (about 5 per person)

2   tablespoons minced tarragon, plus 4 large sprigs for garnish

Place 1 cup yellow tomatoes in blender with water. Puree until smooth. Add remaining tomatoes and yellow pepper; again puree until smooth, then strain through fine mesh sieve. You should get about 2 1/2 cups liquid. Bring a large pot of water to a boil to cook linguine. Place oil in a sauté pan over high heat. Add shallots, garlic, thyme, and oregano. Sauté 3 minutes until fragrant, then deglaze with vodka. Add tomato-pepper puree, cream, and peas. Bring to a boil. Reduce heat and simmer until sauce has thickened. Season with salt and pepper.

Cook linguine. Rinse scallops and pat dry; season with tarragon, salt, and pepper. Heat another sauté pan over high heat. When the sauté pan is almost smokin' hot, place scallops one at a time flat side down to sear in the pan. Let them cook for 3 minutes on one side and then gently turn them over to finish searing. Drain linguine and coat lightly with Tarragon Oil.

 TO PLATE: *Ladle 1/2 cup (4 ounces) of tomato-pepper sauce onto each plate. Divide linguine into 4 portions, twisting with a fork to place a large mound in the center of the plate. Arrange scallops in sauce around linguine and garnish pasta with a tarragon sprig.*

Tarragon Oil

2   cups ice cubes

2   cups cold water

¾   cup tarragon

¼   cup parsley

1   cup olive oil

Bring a small pot of water to a boil. Make an ice bath by placing ice cubes in a bowl with water. Place tarragon and parsley in boiling water. Blanch for 2 minutes. Drain and shock in ice bath, about 5 minutes. Place herbs in blender with oil and puree. Let stand over night. Strain through chinoise. Store tightly covered.

Cioppino

Yield: 6 servings

You will be amazed at how simple this is to cook and how fabulous it looks and tastes. Make sure your shellfish is fresh! If any of the clams or mussels are open, tap them lightly on the countertop and see if they close. If they don't, throw them away.

2 tablespoons olive oil	1 tablespoon kosher salt
3 tablespoons minced garlic	1 teaspoon white pepper
3 tablespoons minced shallots	$\frac{1}{2}$ tablespoon chili flakes
$\frac{1}{2}$ pound rinsed and debearded mussels	1 cup red wine
$\frac{1}{2}$ pound scrubbed Manila clams	6 snow crab clusters
$\frac{1}{2}$ pound peeled and deveined small (31–40 ct) shrimp	1 can (28 ounces) diced tomatoes, pureed in blender
$\frac{1}{2}$ pound diced mahi mahi	2 cups fish stock (p. 2)
2 tablespoons minced thyme	1 pound cooked linguine
2 tablespoons minced oregano	$\frac{1}{2}$ cup basil chiffonade
2 tablespoons minced parsley	$\frac{1}{2}$ cup grated Asiago cheese

In a large stockpot, place oil, garlic, and shallots over high heat. Sauté 2 to 3 minutes, until garlic becomes aromatic. Add mussels, clams, shrimp, and mahi mahi. Cook until pan is almost dry. Add thyme, oregano, parsley, salt, pepper, and chili flakes. Deglaze with wine, then add crab clusters, tomato puree, and fish stock. Bring to a boil. Reduce heat and cook for 4 to 6 minutes, until all clams and mussels are open.

TO PLATE: *Remove crab clusters from broth and arrange in a large serving bowl with bodies in bowl and legs protruding out. Place linguine on top of crab bodies. Pour broth and shellfish over linguine. Garnish with basil chiffonade and cheese.*

Paella

Yield: 4 servings

The spice of this recipe really depends on the chorizo. You may not be able to find it—so spicy Italian sausage can be substituted. Check the flavor of the rice; you may want to add 1 teaspoon of red chili flakes when you add the seafood.

2 tablespoons butter	2 cups long-grain white rice
1 cup finely diced onion	$\frac{1}{2}$ cup white wine
1 teaspoon dried saffron threads	1 pound scrubbed clams
1 can (14.5 ounces) diced tomatoes	1 pound rinsed and debearded mussels
4 cups water	1 pound peeled and deveined small (31–40 ct) shrimp
2 tablespoons olive oil	
2 tablespoons minced garlic	2 tablespoons minced thyme
2 tablespoons minced shallots	2 tablespoons minced oregano
8 ounces diced chicken thighs	2 tablespoons minced parsley
8 ounces ground chorizo	$\frac{1}{2}$ teaspoon kosher salt
	$\frac{1}{4}$ teaspoon white pepper

Melt butter in small saucepan over medium-high heat. Add onion and cook 10 minutes, until tender. Add saffron and cook another 2 minutes. Add diced tomatoes and water and bring to a boil. Reduce heat to a simmer and let saffron steep for 30 minutes.

Place oil in a very large heavy-bottom skillet over high heat. When hot, add garlic and shallots. Cook 2 to 3 minutes, until garlic is aromatic. Add chicken and chorizo and sauté until browned all over. Add rice and sauté another 3 minutes. Deglaze with wine, then add saffron broth. Bring to a boil, then reduce heat to low. Cover and cook 15 minutes.

Uncover and check rice. You may need to add another 1/2 cup of water if rice is dry. Add clams, mussels, shrimp, thyme, oregano, parsley, salt, and pepper. Cook another 5 minutes, until clams and mussels are open, shrimp is opaque, and rice is tender.

 TO PLATE: *This is a great dish to serve family style— right out of the skillet.*

sHeLLfiSh

Shrimp are now abundantly farm raised all over the world—China, Taiwan, Thailand, Ecuador, and Chile—due to incredible demand. They are categorized by colors like white, brown, pink, red, and striped, but the colors are not indicators of what the shrimp may look like. They are harvested and processed immediately onboard ship. Don't be sucked in by grocery store nomenclature. Jumbo shrimp in one store may not be the same size as jumbo shrimp in another store. All shrimp are sold by the number of shrimp per pound, from smallest to largest: 31–40, 16–20, and U10 count (fewer than ten shrimp per pound). Shrimp versus prawn— what's the difference? Spelling and pronunciation, as far as I can tell. According to biological classifications, prawns are freshwater and shrimp are saltwater. Generally speaking, in the United States a prawn is a very large shrimp, ten count per pound and above; the rest are shrimp. Rock shrimp are named for their very hard shells and firm texture that is more lobsterlike than other shrimp.

Pad Thai Shrimp Salad

Yield: 2 cups peanut dressing, 8 servings of salad

The dressing for this salad is spicy! If you are a wimp, decrease the amount of red curry paste to 1 tablespoon. Sweet soy, black sesame seeds, and red curry paste are available in Asian markets.

- $\frac{1}{2}$ cup coconut milk
- $\frac{1}{2}$ cup peanuts, plus 2 tablespoons chopped
- $\frac{1}{2}$ cup rice wine vinegar
- $\frac{1}{4}$ cup soy sauce
- 1 tablespoon sweet soy sauce, plus 4 tablespoons for drizzling
- $\frac{1}{2}$ cup diced red onion
- 1 tablespoon minced garlic
- 2 tablespoons red curry paste
- $\frac{1}{4}$ cup chopped basil
- 2 tablespoons sesame oil
- $\frac{1}{2}$ cup vegetable oil
- 1 package (6.75 ounces) rice noodles
- 2 pounds peeled and deveined medium (16–20 ct) shrimp
- 8 cups mixed field greens
- $\frac{1}{4}$ cup red pepper sesame oil (p. 108)
- 1 tablespoon toasted white sesame seeds (p. 81)
- 1 tablespoon toasted black sesame seeds (p. 81)

Clean and oil surface of gas or charcoal grill, then preheat. Soak eight wooden skewers in water for 30 minutes.

Place coconut milk, 1/2 cup peanuts, vinegar, soy sauce, 1 tablespoon sweet soy sauce, onion, garlic, curry paste, and basil in blender. Puree until smooth. With blender running on medium speed, slowly drizzle in the oils. (If the blender stops incorporating the oils, add a couple of tablespoons of water and resume adding oils.)

Place rice noodles in medium-size bowl. Cover noodles with boiling hot water. This will soften the noodles; it will take 5 to 10 minutes.

Drain the water from the noodles and rinse with cold water to stop softening process. Cover noodles with a damp paper towel.

Divide the shrimp onto the eight skewers. Brush with a little of the peanut dressing. Place on hot grill. Cook 4 to 6 minutes per side, being careful not to burn the shrimp. They are delicate and do not have to be placed over the hottest part of the grill!

Place greens in a large bowl. Place 1/4 cup, more or less to taste, of the dressing over greens and toss to coat.

Place noodles in a large bowl. Toss the noodles with 1/4 cup of dressing, more or less to taste.

TO PLATE: *Place the noodles in the center of each plate in a pile, and arrange the greens in a circle around them, lay shrimp skewer on top of noodles. Drizzle plate with sweet soy and red pepper sesame oil. Top with the extra 2 tablespoons of chopped peanuts and toasted sesame seeds.*

Hoisin-Glazed Shrimp with Udon Noodle Slaw and Snap Pea Vinaigrette

Yield: 2 1/4 cups glaze, 6 servings

Hoisin sauce and plum sauce can be found in the Asian section of most grocery stores or in Asian markets.

$\frac{1}{2}$ cup plum sauce

$\frac{1}{2}$ cup hoisin sauce

$\frac{1}{2}$ tablespoon sambal

$\frac{1}{2}$ cup pineapple juice

1 tablespoon minced gingerroot

1 tablespoon soy sauce

1 tablespoon sesame oil

$\frac{1}{2}$ tablespoon seeded and minced jalapeño

$\frac{1}{2}$ tablespoon minced garlic

2 pounds peeled and deveined medium (16–20 ct) shrimp

Clean surface of gas or charcoal grill, then preheat. In a small bowl whisk all ingredients together, except shrimp, until smooth. Place shrimp in another bowl and toss with 1/2 cup of glaze. Place shrimp on hot grill surface and cook 3 minutes. Turn over, brush with more glaze, and cook another 3 to 5 minutes.

 TO PLATE: *Pour 1/4 cup (2 ounces) Snap Pea Vinaigrette onto each plate and tilt plate to cover base. Place a heaping pile of Udon Noodle Slaw in center of plate. Arrange shrimp on top of noodles.*

Udon Noodle Slaw

Yield: 1 1/4 cups vinaigrette, 6 servings of noodles

$\frac{1}{2}$ cup plum sauce

$\frac{1}{4}$ cup rice wine vinegar

1 tablespoon minced gingerroot

1 tablespoon minced shallots

2 tablespoons lime juice

$\frac{1}{4}$ teaspoon kosher salt

$\frac{1}{8}$ teaspoon white pepper

$\frac{1}{2}$ tablespoon sesame oil

$\frac{1}{4}$ cup vegetable oil

2 packages (22 ounces each) udon noodles

1 cup julienne snap peas

1 cup julienne red pepper

2 small peeled and julienned carrots

Place plum sauce, vinegar, ginger, shallots, lime juice, salt, and white pepper in blender and puree till smooth. With blender running, slowly add oils in a thin stream. Bring a pot of water to a boil. Cook udon noodles for 3 minutes. Drain and rinse with cool water. Combine noodles and julienne vegetables in bowl and toss with vinaigrette to taste.

Snap Pea Vinaigrette

Yield: 2 cups

$\frac{1}{2}$ bunch chopped green onions

$\frac{1}{2}$ seeded and chopped jalapeño

2 cups snap peas

$\frac{3}{4}$ cup rice wine vinegar

$\frac{1}{4}$ cup lemon juice

$\frac{1}{2}$ tablespoon ground ginger

$\frac{1}{2}$ tablespoon wasabi powder

$\frac{1}{2}$ cup pickled ginger

1 tablespoon Dijon mustard

$\frac{1}{2}$ teaspoon kosher salt

$\frac{1}{4}$ teaspoon white pepper

$\frac{1}{4}$ cup sesame oil

$\frac{1}{2}$ cup vegetable oil

Place onions, jalapeño, peas, vinegar, and lemon juice in blender. Puree and pour through fine mesh strainer. Place strained liquid back in blender. Add ginger, wasabi powder, pickled ginger, mustard, salt, and pepper and puree until smooth. With blender running, slowly drizzle in oils in a thin stream.

Curried Shrimp Eggrolls with Jalepeño Dipping Sauce

Yield: 8 eggrolls

You can find eggroll skins in the freezer or refrigerated section of most grocery stores or in Asian markets.

Oil for fryer

2 minced green onions

$\frac{1}{4}$ cup minced yellow onion

1 teaspoon minced garlic

1 seeded and finely diced jalapeño

1 cup cooked finely diced red potato

1 teaspoon dry mustard

1 teaspoon ground ginger

$\frac{1}{2}$ teaspoon cayenne

1 teaspoon curry powder

1 teaspoon cumin

$\frac{1}{4}$ cup mayonnaise

$\frac{1}{2}$ teaspoon kosher salt

$\frac{1}{2}$ pound peeled, deveined, and cooked small (31–40 ct) shrimp

8 egg roll skins

1 egg beaten with 1 tablespoon of water

4 tablespoons sweet soy sauce

2 tablespoons sesame seeds

Preheat fryer to 350°F.

In a small bowl, combine green and yellow onions, garlic, jalapeño, potato, mustard, ginger, cayenne, curry powder, cumin, mayonnaise, salt, and shrimp. Mix very thoroughly.

TO ROLL EGGROLLS: Place one or two skins on lightly floured work surface with one end pointing toward you. With a pastry brush lightly cover entire skin with egg wash. Place 2 tablespoons of filling in center of skin. Be careful not to put too much filling in one skin. Fold bottom flap over filling. Fold each side over bottom flap so that the eggroll skin package looks like an open envelope. Press edges down so there are no air pockets. Roll bottom over top flap and make sure all edges are sealed. It is very important to make sure the edges are sealed. If you don't, the eggrolls will burst while cooking. You may have to roll the eggrolls gently back and forth after filling to obtain a cylindrical shape.

Fry for 5 to 6 minutes until they are hot all the way through.

 TO PLATE: *Cut in half diagonally, drizzle with sweet soy sauce, and garnish with sesame seeds. Serve with warm Jalapeño Dipping Sauce.*

Jalapeño Dipping Sauce

Yield: 1 1/2 cups

Look for Cholula hot sauce in the Mexican food section of the grocery store or your local Mexican market. You can also order it on-line at www.cholula.com.

2 tablespoons sugar

2 tablespoons rice wine vinegar

$\frac{1}{4}$ teaspoon kosher salt

2 tablespoons ketchup

$\frac{1}{2}$ teaspoon Cholula

$1\frac{1}{2}$ cups pineapple juice

$\frac{1}{2}$ teaspoon ground ginger

1 halved jalapeño

1 bay leaf

Whisk all ingredients together in a small saucepan over medium high heat. Slowly bring sauce to a boil, whisking occasionally to prevent sugar from burning. Reduce heat and simmer 10 minutes.

Terminal

Yield: 4 servings

This dish was named after the Terminal Bar, which stood where JAX Fish House in Denver stands today. It was even mentioned in a song by Tom Waits, "Nighthawks Postcards."

Oil for fryer

2 pounds cooked and diced red potatoes

½ cup diced red onion

1 cup diced red pepper

1 cup diced green pepper

½ cup JAX Balsamic Vinaigrette (p. 109)

1 zucchini, sliced diagonally in 1/4-inch-thick pieces

1 yellow squash, sliced diagonally in 1/4-inch-thick pieces

1 quartered portobello mushroom

2 halved Roma tomatoes

4 New York strip steaks (14 ounces each)

1 bunch trimmed and blanched asparagus

12 peeled and deveined medium (16–20 ct) shrimp

Olive oil

Kosher salt and black pepper

1 cup cornmeal

8 shucked East Coast oysters

White pepper

½ batch Andouille Sausage and Crawfish Gumbo (p. 36)

4 whole crawfish

Clean and oil surface of gas or charcoal grill, then preheat. Preheat fryer to 350°F. Combine potatoes, onion, red pepper, and green pepper. Toss with 1/4 cup vinaigrette, or to taste. Toss zucchini, squash, mushroom, and tomatoes in a large bowl with remaining 1/4 cup vinaigrette, or to taste. Brush New York strip steaks, asparagus, and shrimp with olive oil and season with salt and black pepper. Place steak on hot grill surface. Cook to desired temperature. As steak is cooking, rotate zucchini, squash, mushroom, and tomatoes on grill. Cook 3 to 4 minutes per side, until vegetables are slightly charred and softened. When steaks are almost done, grill shrimp and asparagus 2 to 3 minutes per side.

Meanwhile, place 2 tablespoons of olive oil in a large sauté pan over medium-high heat. When hot, add potato mixture and sear on all sides; cook 5 to 8 minutes. Place a small pan over high heat with enough oil to cover the bottom of the pan by one-quarter inch. Place cornmeal in a bowl. Toss oysters in cornmeal. Place cornmeal-crusted oysters in fryer for 3 to 4 minutes and season with salt and white pepper. Place 3 shrimp on each skewer.

TO PLATE: *Place mound of potatoes at top center of plate. Divide vegetables among plates and fan out to the right side of the potatoes. Place steak on top of potatoes. Smother steak in Andouille Sausage and Crawfish Gumbo. Stick shrimp skewer through top center of steak. Garnish plate with fried oysters and crawfish.*

SuRF 'n' TuRf

Some new versions!

Miso-Pomegranate-Glazed Pork and Seared Scallops with Sob

Yield: 3/4 cup glaze, 6 servings pork/scallops

You can find pomegranate juice concentrate in Middle East markets. Miso is fermented soybean paste and can be found in Asian markets or in the Asian section of some grocery stores. There are usually two varieties: white, which is mild flavored; and red, which is stronger.

- $\frac{1}{4}$ **cup pomegranate juice concentrate**
- $\frac{1}{2}$ **cup white miso paste**
- 2 **tablespoons brown sugar**
- 2 **tablespoons soy sauce**
- 2 **tablespoons rice wine vinegar**
- 2 **juniper berries**
- **Pinch cinnamon**
- 1 **bay leaf**
- 1 **clove**
- $2\frac{1}{2}$ **pounds pork tenderloin**
- 12 **large (U10 ct) scallops**
- **Olive oil**
- **Salt**
- **White pepper**

Cut six wooden skewers in half and soak the twelve halves in water for 30 minutes. Clean and oil surface of gas or charcoal and then preheat grill.

Place all ingredients except pork and scallops in a small saucepot and bring to a boil. Reduce heat and simmer until thickened. Brush pork with olive oil and season with salt and pepper. Sear on hot grill surface for 5 to 8 minutes. Turn over, sear other side, and brush with glaze. Move pork tenderloin off direct heat, cover grill, and continue turning and glazing until cooked through, 15 to 20 minutes; this will prevent it from charring too much on one side. Remove pork from grill and let rest 10 minutes.

Meanwhile, place 2 scallops flat on work surface. Pierce two skewers through each scallop, one on the right side and one on the left side. Repeat with remaining scallops to make a total of six "double" skewers. Brush with oil and season with salt and pepper. Place scallops on grill. Sear 2 minutes, turn over, and brush with glaze. Cover and let finish cooking.

 TO PLATE: *Slice pork diagonally in 1/2-inch-thick slices. Ladle 1/3 cup (roughly 2 1/2 ounces) Plum Wine Reduction onto plate. Place 2 Soba Scallion Cakes in back center of plate. Place sautéed snow peas in front of soba cakes. Layer 2 to 3 pork slices from top of soba cakes onto snow peas. Stick scallop skewers through pork slices so they stand up off from pork.*

96

callion Cakes and Plum Wine Reduction

Soba Scallion Cakes

Yield: 6 cakes

If soba noodles stick together after cooking, rinse with a little cool water.

- 1 **pound cooked, drained, and rinsed soba noodles**
- ½ **cup sesame oil**
- 1 **bunch minced scallions**
- 2 **tablespoons flour**
  Kosher salt and white pepper
- 2 **cups snow peas**
- 1 **tablespoon sesame seeds**

Toss soba noodles with 2 tablespoons of sesame oil. Add scallions and flour and mix thoroughly. Divide into 6 portions. Place 2 to 3 tablespoons sesame oil on large flat griddle over medium-high heat. Place several soba noodle cakes on griddle. Press with spatula to flatten. Season with salt and pepper. Let sear on one side for 4 to 5 minutes. Flip and sear on second side. Remove from grill and keep warm. Repeat this process as necessary to finish the cakes, adding more oil as needed. Place 1 tablespoon of sesame oil on griddle. Add snow peas and sesame seeds and cook 3 to 4 minutes until seeds are toasted and snow peas are bright green and just tender.

Plum Wine Reduction

Yield: 4 cups

Make this sauce a day ahead. It is easy but time-consuming.

- 1½ **pounds chicken bones**
- 1½ **pounds veal bones**
- 6 **cloves garlic**
- 2 **halved shallots**
- 2 **cups chopped onion**
- 2 **cups chopped celery**
- 2 **cups peeled and chopped carrots**
- 1 **tablespoon black peppercorns**
- 2 **sprigs thyme**
- 2 **sprigs oregano**
- 1 **bay leaf**
- 1 **gallon water**
- 2 **cups plum wine**

Preheat oven to 375°F. Place chicken and veal bones in roasting pan in oven and roast 30 minutes. Add garlic, shallots, onion, celery, and carrots to pan and roast another 30 minutes, until vegetables are soft and bones are golden brown. Remove from oven. Place bones and vegetables in a large stockpot. Add peppercorns, thyme, oregano, and bay leaf and cover with water. Bring to boil. Reduce heat to a very low simmer and cook 8 hours. Skim foam from top as necessary to remove any impurities. Let sit overnight. Strain and reserve liquid; discard bones and vegetables. Return liquid to pot, let reduce by half. Add plum wine and let reduce by half again.

97

Rockefeller New York Strip with Creole Hollandaise and Gorgonzola Mashers

Yield: 8 servings

To shuck oysters, see tip on page 69. Pernod is an anise-flavored liquor.

Oil for fryer

8 New York strip steaks (10 ounces each)

1 bunch trimmed and blanched asparagus

4 halved Roma tomatoes

Olive oil

Kosher salt for seasoning, plus 1/2 teaspoon for spinach

White pepper for seasoning, plus 1/4 teaspoon for spinach

2 cups cornmeal

2 dozen shucked East Coast oysters

4 tablespoons minced bacon

2 tablespoons minced shallots

2 bunches washed spinach leaves

$\frac{1}{2}$ teaspoon salt

$\frac{1}{4}$ teaspoon pepper

4 tablespoons Pernod

1 tablespoon lemon juice

2 tablespoons butter

Clean and oil surface of gas or charcoal grill, then preheat. Preheat fryer to 350°F. Season steaks, asparagus, and tomatoes with oil, salt, and pepper. Place steaks on grill and cook to desired temperature. Five minutes before steaks are done, grill asparagus and tomatoes, and remove from heat when done.

Place cornmeal in a large bowl. Drain oysters and toss with cornmeal to coat. Place bacon in a large sauté pan over high heat. When it is crispy, add shallots and cook 2 minutes more. Add spinach, salt, and pepper. Deglaze with Pernod. Add lemon juice. Keep turning spinach to wilt evenly, then remove from heat immediately. At the last minute, fry oysters, 3 to 4 minutes until outside is crispy.

 TO PLATE: *Place a large scoop of Gorgonzola Mashers onto each plate. Place asparagus to right of potatoes, and lean steak on top of mashers. Place spinach on top of steak and top spinach with Creole Hollandaise and fried oysters. Garnish plate with grilled tomato halves.*

98

Creole Hollandaise

Yield: 2 cups

You may want to make the creole sauce a day ahead of time and reheat to add to the hollandaise just before serving.

1	tablespoon olive oil
1	small diced green pepper
½	diced red pepper
½	diced onion
2	tablespoons minced garlic
2	tablespoons minced shallots
½	seeded and diced jalapeño
¼	cup white wine
½	cup clam juice
½	cup tomato juice
1	tablespoon Worcestershire sauce
2	teaspoons Cholula
1½	tablespoons lemon juice
1	teaspoon honey
¼	teaspoon kosher salt, plus more for seasoning
¼	teaspoon black pepper
½	teaspoon dried oregano
½	teaspoon dried thyme
½	teaspoon dried basil
1	teaspoon JAX Blackening Spice
2	egg yolks
2	tablespoons cold water
8	ounces clarified butter (p. 32)
	White pepper

TO MAKE THE CREOLE SAUCE: Place oil in a small saucepan over high heat. Add green pepper, red pepper, and onion. Sauté 10 minutes until tender (you may have to reduce the heat). Add garlic, shallots, and jalapeño and sauté 2 to 3 minutes. Increase heat back to high. Deglaze with wine and add clam juice, tomato juice, Worcestershire sauce, Cholula, 1/2 tablespoon lemon juice, honey, 1/4 teaspoon salt, black pepper, oregano, thyme, basil, and JAX Blackening Spice. Bring to a boil. Reduce heat and simmer 15 minutes. Cool sauce. Place in blender and puree until smooth, then pour through fine mesh strainer. Reheat and keep warm.

TO MAKE THE HOLLANDAISE: Bring a small pot of water to a simmer. Place egg yolks and cold water in a small bowl over pot. Whisk egg yolks until they turn pale yellow in color and stiffen slightly. While still whisking, incorporate the clarified butter in a thin stream. Whisk in remaining 1 tablespoon lemon juice and season with salt and white pepper. Whisk in warm creole sauce. Turn off simmering water and keep Creole Hollandaise warm in bowl on top.

Gorgonzola Mashers

Yield: 8 servings

8	large peeled and chopped Idaho potatoes
4	ounces crumbled Gorgonzola cheese
1	cup heavy cream
4	ounces (1 stick) butter
½	cup grated Parmesan cheese
	Kosher salt and white pepper

Cook potatoes in boiling water until tender. Drain and mash with Gorgonzola cheese.

Heat cream and butter until butter has melted. Add to potatoes as necessary to form smooth but still stiff mashed potatoes. Add Parmesan cheese and season with salt and pepper.

Swordfish has gotten a bad rap. It was definitely overfished in the 1980s. Swordfish weighing twelve hundred pounds and measuring fifteen feet were being caught. These fish are solitary; they don't swim in schools and they live for about nine years. For a while, there were very restrictive fishing guidelines. Today, swordfish is slowly coming back as a species and is being carefully watched, so it is okay to buy and eat swordfish. It will probably be expensive and not always available, but it is a great treat. Its flesh is white with pink tinges, and the skin is very tough. It is fished all over the world, and the average size is fifty to one hundred pounds.

SwOrD FiSh

Grilled Swordfish with Cranberry Relish, Braise

Yield: 1 cup cranberry relish, 4 servings of swordfish

- $\frac{1}{4}$ **cup finely diced red onion**
- $\frac{3}{4}$ **cup dried cranberries**
- 2 **tablespoons brown sugar**
- 2 **tablespoons red wine vinegar**
- 2 **tablespoons cider vinegar**
- $\frac{1}{2}$ **teaspoon minced rosemary**
- $\frac{1}{4}$ **teaspoon kosher salt, plus more for seasoning**
- $\frac{1}{8}$ **teaspoon white pepper, plus more for seasoning**
- $\frac{3}{4}$ **cup water**
- $1\frac{1}{2}$ **pounds swordfish, cut into 4 steaks of equal thickness**
- $\frac{1}{2}$ **bunch asparagus**
- **Olive oil**

Preheat oven to 375°F. Clean and oil the surface of a gas or charcoal grill, then preheat.

Place onion, cranberries, brown sugar, red wine vinegar, cider vinegar, rosemary, 1/4 teaspoon salt, 1/8 teaspoon pepper, and water in small sauce-pot. Bring to a boil. Reduce heat to low and simmer until cranberries plump up and all liquid is absorbed, about 30 minutes.

Season swordfish and asparagus with olive oil, salt, and pepper. Place asparagus on baking sheet in oven for 15 to 20 minutes, until tender. Place swordfish on hot grill. Cooking times will vary greatly depending on cut of swordfish steak. Thinner cuts cook quickly and stay moist; thicker cuts take a long time and have a tendency to dry out. If all you can find are thick cuts, you may want to butterfly them.

 TO PLATE: *Place 1 wedge of Apple Potato Rösti at top center of each plate. Place several asparagus spears to the right of the rösti. Place fish on top in center of plate. Spoon Braised Chanterelles and braising liquid over fish and onto plate. Top fish with cranberry relish.*

Braised Chanterelles

Yield: 2 cups

If you can't find chanterelle mushrooms, substitute your favorite type.

- 1 **tablespoon olive oil**
- 1 **tablespoon minced shallots**
- 1 **tablespoon minced garlic**
- 3 **ounces coarsely chopped fresh chanterelle mushrooms (about 1 1/2 cups)**
- $\frac{1}{2}$ **cup chardonnay**
- 1 **tablespoon minced thyme**
- 1 **tablespoon minced rosemary**
- 1 **cup fish stock (p. 2)**
- 2 **tablespoons honey**
- $\frac{1}{2}$ **teaspoon kosher salt**
- $\frac{1}{8}$ **teaspoon white pepper**

Preheat oven to 375°F. Heat oil in a large oven-safe saucepan. Add shallots and garlic and sauté until fragrant. Add mushrooms and sauté until they begin to release liquid. Continue cooking until liquid evaporates and pan is almost dry. Deglaze with chardonnay. Add thyme, rosemary, fish stock, honey, salt, and pepper. Cover pan loosely with foil and let braise in oven for 1 hour.

Apple Potato Rösti

Yield: 1 large potato cake, 4 servings

Rösti is a large potato pancake, crispy on the outside, moist and tender on the inside.

- 3 **slices finely chopped applewood-smoked bacon**
- 3 **medium peeled and grated Idaho potatoes**
- 2 **peeled and grated Granny Smith apples**
- 2 **tablespoons minced rosemary**
- 2 **tablespoons minced thyme**
- $\frac{1}{2}$ **teaspoon kosher salt**
- $\frac{1}{4}$ **teaspoon white pepper**
- 3 **tablespoons butter**

Heat a 10-inch nonstick sauté pan over high heat. Add bacon and render until crispy. Pour off and reserve excess bacon fat. In a large bowl, toss potatoes, apples, rosemary, thyme, salt, and pepper together. Place mixture in hot sauté pan with bacon. Press down to flatten evenly and push apple-potato mixture to edge of pan. Cook over medium heat, about 8 minutes. An even crust will form on the bottom of the mixture.

Now you are going to have to flip it over! Take a plate, platter, or flat lid the same size as the sauté pan. Place it upside down on top of the rösti, so the raw side of the rösti is next to the flat part of the plate. Put your hand in the center of the plate. With your other hand take the handle of the sauté pan and flip the whole thing onto the plate. Place reserved bacon drippings into pan. Slide the rösti back into the pan raw side down (crusted side up). Let cook another 8 minutes or so.

When the rösti is almost finished, dice butter and place around the edge of the rösti so it melts down the pan and seeps into the potatoes. Slide out onto a cutting board and cut into 4 pieces (like a pizza).

101

Cedar-Planked Red Trout over Applewood-Smoked Bacon and Cornbread Stuffin

Yield: 6 servings

Untreated cedar planks can be found in some hardware stores and some specialty cooking equipment stores.

- 6 **sides red trout (8 to 10 ounces each)**
  Olive oil
  Kosher salt and white pepper
- 2 **tablespoons minced parsley**
- 1 **pound green beans**
- 1 **batch JAX Slaw with Honey Fennel Vinaigrette (p. 23)**

Soak three cedar planks in water for 1 hour. Clean and oil surface of gas or charcoal grill, then preheat. Season fish with oil, salt, pepper, and parsley. Place 2 sides of trout on each cedar plank. Place cedar planks directly on charcoal or gas flame. The cedar plank will begin to smoke; leave it there 2 to 5 minutes to get a good smoke rolling. Transfer plank to grill cooking surface. Cover grill and let trout cook on smoking cedar shingle about 5 to 8 more minutes. While that is cooking, blanch green beans in boiling water until tender. Then season them with salt and pepper.

 TO PLATE: *Place large mound of JAX Slaw at top center of each plate. Remove fish from plank and lean it on top of slaw, tail side up. Place Applewood-Smoked Bacon and Cornbread Stuffing and green beans to either side. Slice Hazelnut Basil Butter into 1/4-inch-thick pieces and place 1 or 2 slices on top of fish and 1 on top of hot green beans.*

Applewood-Smoked Bacon and Cornbread Stuffing

Yield: 6 servings

Make cornbread a day ahead, then cut into small one-inch cubes and let air dry.

- 1 **recipe Cornbread, cubed and dried (p. 36)**
- $\frac{1}{4}$ **cup chopped apple-smoked bacon**
- 1 **cup finely diced onion**
- 1 **cup finely diced celery**
- 1 **cup finely diced Granny Smith apples**
- 1 **teaspoon kosher salt**
- 1 **teaspoon black pepper**
- 3 **tablespoons Worcestershire sauce**
- 2 **cups apple cider**

Preheat oven to 350°F. Place cornbread cubes in 13 x 9 x 2-inch baking dish. Place bacon in a medium-size pot and render until crispy. Add onion, celery, and apples to pot and cook until tender, 10 to 15 minutes. Add salt and pepper. Deglaze with Worcestershire sauce and add apple cider. Bring to a boil. Pour over dried cornbread cubes. Toss to coat evenly with liquid. Cover with foil and bake until all liquid is absorbed and stuffing has heated through—about 20 minutes.

...rith Hazelnut Basil Butter

Hazelnut Basil Butter

Yield: 1 log

This compound butter is also good on a grilled steak. To toast hazelnuts, place on a baking sheet in 350°F oven for 10 to 15 minutes, until fragrant.

- $\frac{1}{3}$ **pound (2 sticks) softened butter**
- 1 **tablespoon minced garlic**
- 1 **tablespoon minced shallots**
- 2 **tablespoons Worcestershire sauce**
- 4 **tablespoons chopped basil**
- $\frac{1}{4}$ **cup toasted and coarsely chopped hazelnuts**

Whip all ingredients together in standing mixer set with paddle attachment. Transfer butter mixture to a large piece of waxed paper. Fold waxed paper over and press butter into a log shape. Twist ends of waxed paper and freeze. Slice as needed.

Unfortunately the only trout available to purchase is farm raised. If you want wild trout, you will have to go catch it yourself. Perhaps one of our fine chefs may even agree to take you fly fishing and teach you the basics. Trout have a firm texture and a delicate flavor with tan flesh that can be tinged slightly pink. Trout propagation began as early as the fourteenth century with Dom Pichon, a French monk, and the first trout farm was built in France in 1852. Seth Green started the first American trout farm in Mumford, New York, in 1864. Most of what you will find in supermarkets today is rainbow trout, which in our area have come from farms in Idaho. Trout grow to market size in eight to twelve months. The color of their flesh depends on what they are fed—from red to golden to standard white. Trout is also a very versatile fish that is great for grilling, baking, or roasting.

TrOuT

Tuna is the largest fish in the mackerel family. There are thirteen species of tuna, but not all of them are commercially harvested. Yellowfin is the most abundantly fished and it usually weighs in at about one hundred pounds. These fish are caught in the Pacific in winter and North Atlantic in summer. Their flesh is dark pink to bright red (the best quality is the brightest red), very firm texture, mild flavor, and low-fat content. Tuna should be cooked like any red meat, rare to medium-rare, to keep the meat moist and tender. When you cook the meat all the way through, it tends to be a little dry. It is probably what you will find in your local grocery store and what we recommend for all of our recipes. Albacore is "the white meat tuna." It is also found in grocery stores, a little lighter in color than yellowfin, light pink to dark pink. There is also bigeye tuna, named for the dark red stripe running down the middle (which is an accumulation of myoglobin—stored for energy); they are bigger than yellowfin (two hundred to four hundred pounds), and these fish are caught more easily in winter and have a slightly higher fat content than yellowfin. The Hawaiian name for "tuna" is *ahi*. Yellowfin is what you should look to buy in your local seafood market. Tuna is great grilled or seared rare—just make sure you buy very high-quality or sushi-grade tuna from a reliable source.

104

TuNa

Tuna Poke with Cucumber Salad

Yield: 4 servings

Sushi rice is short-grained and sticky—it can be found in many grocery stores and Asian markets.

- 2 peeled cucumbers
- 1 small peeled and grated carrot
- $\frac{1}{4}$ thinly sliced red onion
- $\frac{1}{2}$ teaspoon sugar
- $\frac{1}{2}$ teaspoon kosher salt
- 2 teaspoons minced mint
- 1 tablespoon sesame oil
- 2 tablespoons rice wine vinegar
  Oil for frying
- 2 large Idaho potatoes
- 2 tablespoons toasted white sesame seed, plus 1 teaspoon for garnish (p. 81)
- 2 tablespoons toasted black sesame seeds, plus 1 teaspoon for garnish (p. 81)
- 2 teaspoons mustard seeds
- 4 tablespoons pickled ginger, plus 2 teaspoons minced
- 2 teaspoons seeded and minced jalapeño
- 2 teaspoons minced cilantro
- 4 tablespoons sweet soy sauce, plus more for garnish
- 1 pound sushi-grade yellowfin tuna, cut into 1/2-inch cubes
- 2 cups mixed greens
- 2 cups cooked and cooled sushi rice

TO MAKE CUCUMBER SALAD: Cut each cucumber in half lengthwise, remove seeds, then cut into diagonal slices 1/4-inch thick and place in a small bowl. Add carrot, onion, sugar, salt, mint, oil, and vinegar. Toss briefly to mix evenly.

TO MAKE GAUFRETTE CHIPS: Preheat fryer to 325°F. Wash and dry potatoes. Place mandoline on waffle cut setting, at approximately 1/8-inch thickness. Place each potato at a 45-degree angle to mandoline and cut one slice. Turn the potato one quarter turn and make another slice. Turn back one quarter turn to original position and slice again. Keep repeating this motion until potato is completely sliced. (Or, if you don't have a mandoline, peel potatoes and slice in half lengthwise. With flat side down on cutting board, slice each potato as thinly as possible.) Place chips in a bowl of cold lemon water to prevent discoloration. Drain chips and pat dry; this will prevent any spattering. Fry chips in two or three batches. Let drain on paper towels and season with salt.

TO MAKE POKE SEED MIX: In a small bowl, combine 2 tablespoons each of black and white sesame seeds, mustard seeds, 2 teaspoons minced pickled ginger, jalapeño, cilantro, and 4 tablespoons of sweet soy sauce. Stir until combined evenly. Add tuna and stir gently to coat.

 TO PLATE: *Arrange 1/2 cup of greens, stems centered on the top center of each plate in an arc that goes from 9 o'clock to 3 o'clock. Arrange some cucumber salad over the top of greens. Fill a dry 1/2-cup measure with sushi rice, press rice down to form cake, and flip cake out onto center of plate. Do the same with the tuna mixture and place tuna on top of rice. Drizzle plate with Wasabi Tobiko Vinaigrette and sweet soy sauce. Top tuna with pickled ginger. Sprinkle the plate with sesame seeds. Stick 5 to 6 chips into rice.*

Wasabi Tobiko Vinaigrette

Yield: 1 1/4 cups

The tobiko caviar gives this dressing a delightful crunch! Tobiko is flying fish roe, or caviar. It comes in wasabi flavor. You should be able to order it from your local fish counter. Another small egg caviar may be substituted. If you use black, rinse it first and be careful not to crush it when whisking in.

$\frac{1}{4}$ **cup minced pickled ginger**

2 tablespoons rice wine vinegar

2 tablespoons wasabi powder

1 tablespoon minced shallots

$\frac{1}{4}$ **cup minced green onion**

1 tablespoon sesame oil

$\frac{1}{2}$ **cup vegetable oil**

$\frac{1}{4}$ **cup wasabi tobiko caviar**

105

Place ginger, vinegar, wasabi powder, shallots, green onion, and sesame oil in blender. Puree on medium-high setting until smooth. Add vegetable oil slowly, in a thin stream, while blender is on medium-high setting. Remove dressing from blender. Place in bowl and whisk in caviar.

"SASHIMI IN TAILS."
—BILL ST. JOHN,
ROCKY MOUNTAIN NEWS

Chipotle Charred Tuna with Avocado Salad, Green Onion Potato Cake, and Baked Lime Aioli

Yield: 4 servings

Mizuna is a feathery, delicate salad green from Japan. Frisée is a curly-leaved green from the chicory family.

- 4 large peeled and boiled Idaho potatoes
- $\frac{1}{2}$ bunch minced scallions
- $\frac{1}{4}$ cup heavy cream
- $\frac{1}{2}$ teaspoon kosher salt
- $\frac{1}{8}$ teaspoon white pepper
- 1 can (7 ounces) chipotle chile in adobo
- $1\frac{1}{2}$ pounds tuna, cut into 4 square pieces
- 2 tablespoons olive oil
- 1 cup mizuna
- 1 cup frisée
- $\frac{1}{2}$ cup beurre blanc (p. 1)
- 1 peeled and diced avocado
- 2 tablespoons brunoise red onion
- 2 tablespoons brunoise red pepper

Place potatoes in food mill or ricer; it should yield about 8 cups. Gently fold in scallions, cream, salt, and pepper. Using a 1/4-cup measure or ice cream scoop, form into 12 cakes and set aside.

Place chilies and adobo sauce in blender or food processor. Puree until smooth and then strain. Coat tuna with puree. Place 1 tablespoon of olive oil in a sauté pan over high heat. When almost smokin' hot, add tuna. Sear on one side, flip, and sear on the other side. For rare seared tuna, remove from heat at this point. If you prefer medium-rare seared tuna, continue searing on all sides.

Place remaining tablespoon of olive oil on griddle over high heat. Place potato cakes on hot griddle and cook about 3 minutes per side.

Baked Lime Aioli

Yield: 3/4 cup

TO BAKE LIMES OR LEMONS: Bake limes or lemons in an oven-safe container at 350°F for 1 hour. Let cool. Squeeze out juice.

- 1 pasteurized egg yolk
- 1 tablespoon mashed roasted garlic (p. 3)
- 3 baked and juiced limes
- $\frac{1}{4}$ teaspoon kosher salt
- $\frac{1}{8}$ teaspoon white pepper
- $\frac{1}{2}$ cup olive oil

Place egg yolk, garlic, lime juice, salt, and pepper in the bowl of a food processor and blend until pale yellow in color. With food processor running, slowly add oil in a thin stream. Aioli should be the consistency of thin mayonnaise.

TO PLATE: *Mix mizuna and frisée together and place a fourth of the mixture in the center of each plate. Place 3 tablespoons of Baked Lime Aioli around greens. Place potato cake on top of greens and tuna on top of potato cake. Pour beurre blanc over tuna and top with avocado. Garnish the plate with brunoise red onion and red pepper.*

Tuna Niçoise Salad with Lemon Thyme Vinaigrette

Yield: 4 servings

If you ever have tuna left over—this is a great way to use it up! Haricots verts are very small green beans. Caperberries are large-stemmed capers imported from Spain.

- 1$\frac{1}{2}$ pounds tuna
- Olive oil
- Kosher salt and white pepper
- 2 chopped romaine lettuce hearts
- 4 Roma tomatoes, sliced in 1/4-inch-thick pieces
- 1 cup niçoise olives
- $\frac{1}{2}$ pound haricots verts, blanched
- 4 sliced hard-boiled eggs
- $\frac{1}{2}$ cup caperberries
- 1 pound cooked and sliced red potatoes
- Freshly ground black pepper

Clean and oil surface of gas or charcoal grill, then preheat. Coat the tuna with olive oil and season with salt and white pepper. Place tuna on hot grill and cook to desired temperature, 3 to 4 minutes per side for rare. Cool slightly then cut into 1/2-inch-thick slices. In a large bowl, dress romaine with 1/4 cup Lemon Thyme Vinaigrette.

 TO PLATE: *Divide tossed romaine between four large dinner plates. Starting at the top of the plate and working your way around in a clockwise motion, arrange the tomatoes, olives, haricots verts, eggs, caperberries, and potatoes. Arrange 3 to 4 slices of tuna on top of each salad. Drizzle a little more dressing over tuna and vegetable garnishes. Season with salt and black pepper.*

Lemon Thyme Vinaigrette

Yield: 1 1/4 cups

- $\frac{1}{2}$ cup roasted shallots, plus 1 cup reserved oil (p. 3)
- 1 zested and juiced lemon
- $\frac{1}{4}$ cup minced thyme
- 1 tablespoon minced garlic
- 1 tablespoon Dijon mustard
- 1 tablespoon sherry vinegar

Place shallots, lemon, thyme, garlic, mustard, and vinegar in blender. Puree until smooth. With blender running on medium speed, slowly drizzle in roasted shallot oil.

Filet Mignon of Tuna with JAX Balsamic Vinaigrette

Yield: 8 servings

This is an all-time JAX favorite. The quality and cut of tuna is very important to this dish. Try to get four square pieces, about the size of a piece of filet mignon. Also make sure there is very little sinew (white fibers that run through the tuna) in it.

- 3 **pounds cooked and diced red potatoes**
- ½ **cup diced red pepper**
- ½ **cup diced green pepper**
- ¼ **cup diced red onion**
- 2 **tablespoons olive oil, plus more to season asparagus**
- ¼ **cup JAX Balsamic Vinaigrette**
  Kosher salt and white pepper
- 1 **bunch trimmed asparagus**
- ⅓ **cup wasabi powder**
- 2 **tablespoons lime juice**
- 3 **pounds sushi-grade yellowfin tuna, cut into 8 square pieces**
- 1 **cup beurre blanc (p. 1)**
- ½ **cup sweet soy sauce**
- ½ **cup pickled ginger**
- 1 **teaspoon toasted white sesame seeds (p. 81)**
- 1 **teaspoon toasted black sesame seeds (p. 81)**

TO COOK THE HASH BROWNS: In a small bowl, mix together the potatoes, red pepper, green pepper, and onion. Heat 1 tablespoon of the olive oil in a large sauté pan over medium-high heat. Add potato mixture to pan. Sear potatoes on all sides and cook until peppers are tender, 12 to 15 minutes. Toss with JAX Balsamic Vinaigrette and season with salt and white pepper. Keep warm.

Bring pot of water to a boil and blanch asparagus for 3 to 5 minutes, until bright green and tender. Season warm asparagus with olive oil, salt, and pepper.

TO MAKE WASABI BALLS: Place wasabi powder in a small bowl. Add lime juice a little at a time and mix with your fingers or a fork until a paste is formed that is the consistency of play dough. Form into 8 small balls.

TO SEAR THE TUNA: Place remaining tablespoon of olive oil in a sauté pan over high heat. Season the tuna with salt and pepper. Place one side of tuna down in very hot pan. If your pan is not hot enough, the tuna will stick. The oil should be almost at its smoking point. Let the tuna sear on that side for approximately 2 to 3 minutes. It should turn a dark golden brown on the edges. Flip tuna over to opposite side and let sear another 2 minutes. That is a rare-seared tuna; if you would like a medium-rare-seared tuna, just keep searing each of the six sides.

 TO PLATE: *Place wasabi paste balls on one edge of each plate. Divide potatoes and place in the center of each of the plates. Divide asparagus into equal portions and place on plates with ends of asparagus in center of potatoes. Place tuna on top of asparagus ends. Pour 2 tablespoons of beurre blanc on top of each piece of tuna. Drizzle tuna and plate with sweet soy sauce and red pepper sesame oil. Place a little pickled ginger on top of each tuna and garnish with sesame seeds.*

TO MAKE THE RED PEPPER SESAME OIL: Place 1/2 cup of red peppers and mustard in a blender. Add water and puree until smooth. With the blender running, slowly add the sesame and vegetable oils in a thin stream. Strain and pour into a squeeze tube.

JAX Balsamic Vinaigrette

Yield: 3/4 cup

2 tablespoons chopped red onion	**1** tablespoon minced garlic
$\frac{1}{2}$ teaspoon dried oregano	**$\frac{1}{4}$** cup balsamic vinegar
$\frac{1}{2}$ teaspoon dried basil	**$\frac{1}{2}$** cup olive oil
$2\frac{1}{2}$ tablespoons Dijon mustard	Kosher salt and white pepper

Place the onion, oregano, basil, mustard, garlic, and vinegar in a food processor or blender and puree until smooth. With the blender running slowly, incorporate oil in a thin stream. Season with salt and pepper.

Grilled Wahoo with Sweet Corn Broth, Pine Nut Risotto, and Pesto

Yield: 6 servings

2¼ pounds wahoo, cut into 6 equal pieces
Olive oil
Kosher salt and white pepper

Clean and oil surface of gas or charcoal grill, then preheat.
Brush fish with olive oil and season with salt and pepper.
Place fish on hot grill and let cook 3 to 5 minutes. Flip and
let cook another 3 to 5 minutes. Remove from heat.

 TO PLATE: *Ladle 1/2 cup (4 ounces)
of Sweet Corn Broth into each bowl.
Place 1/2 cup of Pine Nut Risotto in
center of bowl. Drizzle Pesto over risotto
and broth. Place fish on top of risotto.
Top fish with corn relish.*

110

Sweet Corn Broth

Yield: 4 cups

One cup of the Sweet Corn Broth is for the Pine Nut
Risotto. The remaining 3 cups are for the main dish.

8   ears corn
2   tablespoons olive oil
1   tablespoon minced garlic
2   tablespoons minced shallots
1   small finely diced onion
1   cup finely diced celery
5   cups water
½   teaspoon kosher salt, plus more for seasoning
¼   teaspoon white pepper, plus more for seasoning
¼   cup basil chiffonade
1   tablespoon butter
1   small finely diced red pepper
1   tablespoon honey

TO MAKE CORN BROTH: Cut kernels from corn cobs and
set aside. Heat oil in a large stockpot and add garlic, shallots,
onion, and celery. Sauté 12 to 15 minutes, until vegetables
are translucent. Add water, corn, 1/2 teaspoon of the salt,
and 1/4 teaspoon of the white pepper and bring to a boil.
Reduce heat and simmer 10 minutes. Add basil chiffonade.
Strain and reserve broth and corn mixture separately.
Reheat broth and check seasonings.

TO MAKE CORN RELISH: Melt butter over medium-high
heat in a saucepan. Add red pepper and cook until tender,
10 minutes. Add reserved corn mixture and honey, heat
through, and season with salt and white pepper.

Pine Nut Risotto

Yield: 3 cups, 6 servings

See tip on page 39 for how to toast pine nuts.

- 1 tablespoon olive oil
- 1 tablespoon minced garlic
- 1 tablespoon minced shallots
- 1 cup arborio rice
- $\frac{1}{4}$ cup white wine
- 1 cup Sweet Corn Broth
- 4 cups hot fish stock (p. 2)
- $\frac{1}{2}$ cup toasted pine nuts
- 2 tablespoons basil chiffonade
- $\frac{1}{4}$ cup grated Asiago cheese
- $\frac{1}{4}$ cup heavy cream
- $\frac{1}{2}$ teaspoon kosher salt
- $\frac{1}{4}$ teaspoon white pepper
- 2 tablespoons butter

Place oil in a large saucepan over high heat. Add garlic, shallots, and rice and sauté 3 to 4 minutes. Deglaze with wine and add 1 cup Sweet Corn Broth. Reduce heat to medium and cook until almost all of the liquid has been absorbed into the rice, stirring frequently. Add 1 cup fish stock. Continue cooking until almost all of the liquid has been absorbed, stirring frequently. Continue to add hot fish stock, 1 cup at a time, until rice is tender and creamy. Stir in pine nuts, basil, cheese, cream, salt, pepper, and butter. Continue stirring until cheese and butter have melted.

Pesto

Yield: 3/4 cup

- 1 cup chopped basil
- $\frac{1}{4}$ cup toasted pine nuts
- $\frac{1}{2}$ zested and juiced lemon
- $1\frac{1}{2}$ tablespoons roasted garlic, plus 1/2 cup oil (p. 3)
- $\frac{1}{4}$ cup grated Asiago cheese
- $\frac{1}{4}$ teaspoon kosher salt
- $\frac{1}{4}$ teaspoon white pepper

Combine basil, pine nuts, lemon, garlic, cheese, salt, and pepper in food processor and pulse to blend. Slowly add oil in a thin stream with food processor running. Pour into a squeeze tube.

Wahoo (like every other fish caught off the coasts of Hawaii) has another Hawaiian name, *ono*. This fish is in the mackerel family, as is mahi mahi, marlin, and tuna. They grow to eight to thirty pounds and have silver skin and no scales. The flesh is pale pink, the texture is very firm, and the flavor is mild. These fish are great grilled or pan roasted.

WaHoO (oNo)

Walleye Tostada with Black Bean Hummus, Cilantro Lime Vinaigrette, and Charre

Yield: 6 servings

Oil for frying
6 corn tortillas
Kosher salt and white pepper
1 egg
1 cup buttermilk
$2\frac{1}{4}$ pounds walleye pike, cut into 1-inch-wide strips
2 cups cornmeal
1 head washed and chopped romaine lettuce
$\frac{1}{4}$ cup Cilantro Lime Vinaigrette
$\frac{1}{4}$ cup crème fraîche (p. 2)
6 Roma tomatoes, sliced in 1/4-inch-thick pieces
2 peeled avocados, sliced in 1/4-inch pieces

Preheat fryer to 375°F. Fry tortillas until crisp and drain on paper towels. Season with salt and pepper. In a small bowl, beat egg with buttermilk. Dip walleye into buttermilk mixture and then into a bowl of cornmeal. Toss to coat. Fry walleye in small batches until golden and crisp. Season with salt and pepper. In a medium-size bowl, toss romaine with 1/4 cup Cilantro Lime Vinaigrette.

 TO PLATE: *Place a small dollop of Black Bean Hummus on center of each plate. Spread a layer of hummus on tostada shell (fried tortilla) and place on top of hummus dollop already on plate. Place tossed romaine on tortilla. Top with Charred Tomato Salsa. Place fish on top of salsa. Drizzle plate with crème fraîche. Garnish with fresh tomato and avocado slices.*

Black Bean Hummus

Yield: 2 1/4 cups

This is a southwestern twist on a Middle Eastern favorite.

1 cup black beans, soaked in water overnight
2 tablespoons roasted garlic (p. 3)
$\frac{1}{4}$ cup finely diced red onion
$\frac{1}{4}$ cup minced green onion
$\frac{1}{2}$ teaspoon cumin
$\frac{1}{4}$ teaspoon Chimayo chili powder
$\frac{1}{2}$ zested and juiced lemon
$\frac{1}{2}$ zested and juiced lime
2 tablespoons tahini
$\frac{1}{2}$ teaspoon kosher salt
$\frac{1}{8}$ teaspoon white pepper

Drain beans and place them in a small saucepot. Cover with water by 3 inches and cook until tender, 2 to 3 hours; add more water as needed. Drain off liquid, rinse beans, and cool. Place beans in food processor with remaining ingredients. Puree until smooth. It may be necessary to add 1 to 2 tablespoons of water to smooth out the puree.

112

Also called yellow pike, though not at all related to pike, walleye are small, delicate fish and are actually in the perch family. If you ever find a whole fish, don't let the cloudy eyes fool you. Cloudy eyes on most fish are an indication of poor handling or age, but even the freshest walleyes have cloudy eyes.

waLLeYe

Cilantro Lime Vinaigrette
Yield: 1 1/2 cups

- 1 **bunch chopped cilantro**
- 1 **zested and juiced lime**
- 2 **tablespoons honey**
- 1 **tablespoon chopped garlic**
- 1 **tablespoon chopped shallots**
- 1 **tablespoon Dijon mustard**
- 2 **tablespoons red wine vinegar**
- $\frac{3}{4}$ **cup olive oil**
- **Kosher salt and white pepper**

Place all ingredients in blender except oil. Puree until smooth. With blender running slowly, drizzle in oil. Season with salt and pepper.

Charred Tomato Salsa
Yield: 1 1/2 cups

- 5 **grilled Roma tomatoes**
- 1 **zested and juiced lime**
- $\frac{1}{2}$ **small finely diced red onion**
- 1 **seeded and finely diced jalapeño**
- $\frac{1}{2}$ **bunch minced cilantro**
- 1 **tablespoon sherry vinegar**
- 1 **tablespoon olive oil**
- $\frac{1}{2}$ **teaspoon kosher salt**
- $\frac{1}{4}$ **teaspoon white pepper**
- $\frac{1}{2}$ **teaspoon cumin**
- $\frac{1}{2}$ **tablespoon ancho chili powder**

Place tomatoes in food processor and pulse twice to coarsely chop. Do not puree! Transfer tomatoes into a large bowl and add remaining ingredients. Mix thoroughly. Chill.

TO GRILL TOMATOES:
Place tomatoes on cleaned, oiled, hot charcoal or gas grill and cook until blistered on all sides.

113

Web Sites for Hard-to-Find Ingredients

asiamex.com (plum sauce, hoisin sauce, sambal, jasmine rice, basmati rice, wasabi, sweet soy sauce, soba noodles, udon noodles, curry pastes, masa pickled ginger)

cajunmarket.com (andouille sausage)

caviarexpress.biz (caviar)

cholula.com (Cholula)

dibruno.com (pancetta, prosciutto, andouille sausage)

crawfish.cc (crawfish, andouille sausage, oysters)

earthy.com (pine nuts, sesame seeds, arborio rice, basmati rice, jasmine rice, beluga lentils, curry pastes)

Indianharvest.com (beluga lentils)

jaxfishhousedenver.com (JAX contact information, JAX Blackening Spice, JAX Old Bay Seafood Seasoning)

jaxfishhouseboulder.com (JAX contact information, JAX Blackening Spice, JAX Old Bay Seafood Seasoning)

katagiri.com (miso paste)

lintonsseafood.safeshopper.com (softshell crabs, oysters, lobsters)

lighthousedeli.com (oysters, crabs)

lilsalseafood.com (oysters)

specialcheese.com (manchengo, queso fresco)

theseamarket.com (lobsters, shrimp, crabs, shellfish)

worldspice.com (ancho chili powder, cardamom pods, saffron threads, juniper berries, pequin chili, filé powder)

brunoise—small dice, 1/8- to 1/16-inch square.

caramelize—to cook long enough to brown natural sugars in foods like onions.

chiffonade—to lay leafy greens or herbs flat, then roll like a cigar and finely slice.

chinois—a conical, very fine mesh sieve.

chop—to cut into large pieces, roughly the same size.

deglaze—to release little browned bits from bottom of pan after sautéing meats or vegetables by adding liquid, usually wine or stock.

dice—to cut into small cubes, 1/4-inch square.

dredge—to coat food with dry ingredient such as flour or bread crumbs.

food mill—a type of mechanical sieve with a crank operated curved blade, used to puree soft foods.

French knife—a large blade, wide at one end, coming to a tip at the other end, usually 8 to 14 inches long.

julienne—to cut in long thin strips 1/8-inch thick.

mandoline—a piece of cooking equipment used to slice, julienne, and waffle cut to a uniform thickness or consistency.

reduce—to boil a liquid until the amount of liquid is reduced by evaporation.

render—to release fat from meat by cooking, then clarifying the drippings.

ricer—a piece of cooking equipment that looks similar to a garlic press; it is used with soft cooked foods that are pushed through a perforated container to produce strings of food about the diameter of a grain of rice.

slurry—a thick mixture of a dry ingredient and a wet ingredient, such as dry spice and oil.

squeeze tube—a cylindrical plastic container about 6 inches tall and with a narrow tip, used to paint sauces onto plates of food.

sweat—to cook vegetables without coloring in a small amount of oil until they soften and release their liquid, and then cover and let them steam in their own juices.

Resources

Bittman, Mark. *Fish—The Complete Guide to Buying and Cooking*. New York: Macmillan General Reference, 1994.

Bolourchi, Mark. "Caviar, the perfect pearls of nature." Available online at www. wines.com/caviar/pearls.

Conway, Linda Glick. *The Professional Chef*. 5th ed. New York: Van Nostrand Reinhold, 1991.

Guide Book to New Zealand Commercial Fish Species. New Zealand Fishing Industry Board, 201 South Main, Suite 900, Salt Lake City, Utah 84111, 1981.

Lee, Mercedes. *Seafood Lovers Almanac*. Quebec: National Audubon Society, 2000.

McClane, A. J. *The Encyclopedia of Fish Cookery*. New York: Holt, Rinehart, and Winston, 1977.

Peterson, James. *Fish and Shellfish*. New York: William Morrow, 1996.

The Seafood Handbook 1989. Seattle: Selling Seafood, Seafood Business.

Index

119